Financial Intimacy

Financial Intimacy

How to Create a Healthy Relationship
with Your Money and Your Mate

Jacquette M. Timmons

CHICAGO
REVIEW
PRESS

Library of Congress Cataloging-in-Publication Data
Timmons, Jacquette M.
    Financial intimacy : how to create a healthy relationship with
your money and your mate / Jacquette M. Timmons.
        p. cm.
    Includes bibliographical references.
    ISBN 978-1-55652-775-3 (pbk.)
    1. Couples—Finance, Personal. 2. Finance, Personal.
3. Couples—Finance, Personal—Case studies. I. Title.

    HG179.T5127 2009
    332.0240086'5—dc22
                                                    2009012508

Cover design: TG Design
Cover image: Shutterstock
Interior design: Pamela Juárez

Published by Chicago Review Press, Incorporated
814 North Franklin Street
Chicago, Illinois 60610
ISBN 978-1-55652-775-3
Printed in the United States of America
5 4 3 2 1

*For my mother, Fontilla Timmons, who in words
and deeds lives out the mantra she espouses:
"Dance to your own beat." Mommy, your instruction
and ever-present example have sustained me at
more times and in more ways than you know.*

and

*In loving memory of my dear friend, Rayes "Deno"
Moss. The brother I never had and the best guy
friend a girl could ever have. Even from heaven, you
continue to teach me. I miss you terribly.*

Contents

Introduction

$\mathcal{J}$ deal with money and the issues it creates in people's lives every day. I work as a financial coach and trainer, providing one-to-one counseling and presenting, throughout the country, workshops on money management and the connection between money and relationships. My profession gives me an insider's perspective on how money shows up in people's lives in general, and how it magnifies the complex and sometimes contradictory nature of romantic relationships in particular.

In 2003, the death of one of my dearest friends, followed by the death of a good friend's father two months later, precipitated one of my "A-ha!" moments about the intersection of love and money. Their deaths brought to my attention a pattern I had not noticed before. Once I became aware of it, I seemed to recognize it everywhere, personally and professionally—with clients, workshop attendees, and friends—and it piqued my curiosity. It became apparent to me that many college-educated, savvy, and otherwise smart professional women do not think about discussing personal finances, *in detail and in depth*, with their mates.

Nadia, a former coaching client of mine, is one example. On paper, she is the epitome of financial success. She has an exciting career, earns nearly half a million dollars a year, and has a sizable savings account and investment portfolio. Her issues with money have less to do with numbers and more to do with her emotions. She fears ending up like her brother, who is financially "strapped and trapped," and doesn't see how this fear is stunting the growth of her relationship with her live-in boyfriend of two years. She never imagined that all the fights she had with him about money stemmed from her fear of becoming like her brother. Through our work, she started to realize that her financial destiny is not set in her DNA. Once she understood that she consciously makes different choices than her brother does, she realized that her fear was unfounded. As a result, she began to communicate differently with her boyfriend about money.

Jaimee, a workshop attendee, is another example. She has been divorced twice and is a bit gun-shy about getting married again. She and her first husband had joint checking and savings accounts. She soon noticed frequent ATM withdrawals and thought it was rather odd, but was satisfied with his answers that he was helping one or another of his needy family members or friends. Eventually she discovered the real reason for his frequent withdrawals was a gambling habit. Her second husband seemed perfectly reasonable when it came to money, but they did not commingle their money—mostly because she was afraid of attaching her lingering debt from her first husband to him. When his business experienced a few lean years, she picked up the slack and worked harder to contribute to the family income. Ironically, as soon as his business took off and was doing well again, he wanted out of the marriage. Now she is single once more and wonders if she'll ever be able to trust a man with her heart and her money again.

Even though the details of these women's stories vary, they share a lot in common. Instead of seeing isolated events, I saw women who, despite being college-educated professionals and financially skillful in many regards, made the same financial mistake.

As I widened my focus beyond these women, it became clearer to me that their experiences with money and love were actually a microcosm of many other women, including myself! Our differences are stark: we are women of different partnership statuses (single, living with someone, married, divorced, widowed); we are straight or gay; come from a variety of family backgrounds, races, and religions; have attended college and post-graduate schools across the country; and work in a variety of professions. But so are our similarities, beginning with the fact that our parents' efforts and the civil rights and women's movements all played a part in paving the way for us to experience academic, professional, and financial success. Yet many of us are failing when it comes to managing money's emotional impact on our relationships. How can this be? What's the cause of this interesting and perplexing duality?

With my personal and professional curiosity amplified, I set out to discover just why my peers and I were ill equipped to talk about money with the very people we should be communicating with, why we were unable to effectively handle the conflict money can cause in our relationships, and perhaps most important, what it takes to create financial intimacy with our mates.

I wondered, if you can "bring home the bacon and fry it up in the pan," as that famous commercial during the women's movement advocated, then why does a chasm exist between most twenty-first-century couples concerning finances? And if you're single, like me, what signs do you look for while dating to ensure financial compatibility? What questions do you consider, and when is it appropriate to ask these questions?

From listening to my coaching clients, workshop attendees, and friends, it is apparent that many couples only have surface-level conversations about money. They do not *really* talk about it, despite sharing pillows, possibly a few tears, and other life-shaping and bonding experiences. Not only are some couples in the dark about how much their respective partners earn, save, invest, and spend, a greater number of couples are clueless about each other's financial histories, expectations, fears, and beliefs.

For all the progress we've achieved as a society, we are woefully behind in terms of our attitudes and actions when it comes to couples talking with transparency about money. This is due to the fact that most people grew up in households that considered it gauche to discuss money. You didn't talk about it within your family unit, and it was understood to be distasteful to discuss money with friends or even with your mate! Money was deemed to be a private and individual matter.

The financial concerns and emotional needs of college-educated, professional women born in the 1960s and 1970s have ushered in the need for a new model. Women of this generation have a desire to proactively choose how money will influence their relationships, especially if they have experienced the ill effects that accompany the "don't talk about money" taboo: broken purses and wounded hearts. But they very often lack the tools to do so.

I wrote *Financial Intimacy* to address that sweet spot where the relationships you have with yourself, your money, and your mate converge. Before this book, there was "Women, Money, and Romance," a workshop I created as a platform to answer what I perceived as a silent cry for help. The two-hour experiential (not lecture-based) workshop was designed around thirteen questions and six real-life case studies. I chose this format to ensure a highly interactive session, and for two more reasons: I believe that before you can effectively engage your mate in a constructive conversation about money, you must first be aware of your own habits, expectations, fears, and beliefs with respect to money; and the case studies allowed everyone to learn from the myriad issues and challenges others had actually faced. Participants related to these stories either because of the similarity to their own lives or because the universal lesson embedded in each case study resonated with them personally.

I presented the first "Women, Money, and Romance" workshop during Women's History Month in 2005. Subsequent sessions as well as informal discussion groups made it clear that I had struck a deep nerve. It seemed that each workshop, despite being two hours in length, was never long enough. The issues that the women wanted to discuss, share, and vent about seemed never-ending, thus further piquing my curiosity to learn even more about the love and money connection.

My journey to find additional answers led to an interesting discovery: regardless of our family environments, almost none of us were taught how to talk about love *and* money.

The truth about our circumstances prompted me to dig even deeper and look for answers in the context of what has transpired culturally in the last forty years. As I searched, I found a clue in the most unlikely of places—my Brooklyn neighborhood.

When people ask me where I live and I mention Park Slope, I get one of two reactions: eyes that light up or eyes that roll, both for the same reason, ironically. In December 2006, *Natural Home* magazine named my beloved neighborhood one of America's ten best neighborhoods. It did not always hold this distinction, certainly not when I moved into the area in 1985.

Fortunately for me, the block on which I lived back then was considered one of the nicer ones, but it was bordered by an avenue that you didn't walk down after dark. Paradoxically, this juxtaposition gave the neighborhood its edgy appeal—the perfect place for college students like me at the time and bohemians of all types. Today, that avenue is no longer lined with the bodegas that sold more illegal goods than legal, nor is it primarily occupied by immigrants and first-generation American families. Instead, you will find trendy restaurants and bars and chic boutiques. Likewise, many of the immigrants of old have been replaced by new domestic "immigrants," otherwise known as well-to-do transplants from Manhattan.

The big picture of the gentrification that was under way in my neighborhood was not initially evident to me. At first, what I noticed was a store here or there closing and something else opening up in its place. A cozy coffee shop, the first of its kind at the time, replaced the old-style pharmacy down the block from my current apartment and across the street from the Brooklyn Conservatory of Music. My favorite Greek diner closed and was followed by a string of commercial occupants—now it's an ATM center for a major bank. A Spanish restaurant, a neighborhood staple for over thirty years, was replaced by a chain drugstore.

The proverbial "trees" were in focus, but I had no sight of the "forest." Though Park Slope's physical and residential landscape was being altered right before my eyes, the pace in the beginning was such that it was almost imperceptible. Mine was the classic case of being too close to see.

To miss the parallel between the gentrification of my neighborhood and realizing financial intimacy is to overlook the relationship between proximity and perspective. When you are "too close to see," you often notice the clues you should have been paying attention to long after the fact.

Søren Kierkegaard was right: "Life can only be understood backwards, but it must be lived forwards." It's funny what you recognize after the fact but don't notice when you are living through it. I imagine this is how our parents, who were coming into adulthood in the 1960s and 1970s, must feel as they look back to that time in our history. Yes, the United States was undergoing such significant changes politically, socially, economically, and culturally, that one would be hard-pressed to say he or she didn't recognize the changes afoot. But no one could have ever imagined the magnitude of those changes and how they'd reverberate all the way through to the twenty-first century—all the way through to you and me, their daughters biologically and symbolically.

Forty years ago, the civil rights movement dismantled Jim Crow laws and granted black Americans in the South the right to vote. Today, the president is a black man. Forty years ago, Second Wave feminists fought for gender equality and equal pay. Today, Third Wave feminists have expanded the fight beyond equality issues to focus on issues of choice. Forty years ago, your race was white, black, or "other," and homosexuality was considered aberrant and not deemed to be a viable orientation. Multiculturalism and diversity awareness didn't exist to the degree that they do today.

Similarly, the landscape of personal finance has shifted quite a bit. Forty years ago, you banked at your local bank where the branch manger knew you by name, few people had credit cards, and investing in the stock market was the domain of the "rich." Today, most banking transactions are done online, almost everyone has a credit card, and mutual funds have made investing accessible for Joe and Jane on Main Street. Forty years ago, you were almost destined to work for the same employer for at least twenty-five years, and your employer acknowledged your loyalty by investing for your retirement via a defined-benefit plan. Today young baby boomers have on average ten jobs in a lifetime, and investing for your retirement is primarily your responsibility via self-directed defined-contribution plans.[1]

Clearly, the list of changes between then and now is much longer. But what this list illustrates is that the political, sociocultural, and economic environment looked very different forty years ago, and it will look different forty years hence. Nevertheless, there are some things about life that remain constant regardless of the changes happening around us. People will meet, they will marry (or demonstrate some other such form of commitment), and they will create families that may include children. They will experience the accompanying vicissitudes of life. And money will be there at each moment of every day, playing its role, sometimes in the shadows and at other times front and center, but always there.

Think about your life for a quick moment. What immediately comes to mind as you ponder the role money has played in it? What aspects seem so obvious today that may have previously been imperceptible? What comes to mind when you consider how the intersection of love and money has played out in your romantic relationships?

Forty years ago, financial intimacy, or managing money's emotional impact on our romantic relationships, was not a part of our personal and financial vernacular. But the need for it was just as ubiquitous then as it is today. For many of us, our parents were too busy living out and living through unprecedented changes to focus on financial intimacy for themselves, let alone to possess the vision to see that it—like all of the other life skills they taught us by instruction or example—might be something we would need to learn and cultivate.

It's hard to intentionally teach what you don't know or what seems socially irrelevant at a particular time, so I am not blaming our parents for not equipping us with a toolkit to help us manage the intersection of love and money. But there's no escaping the fact that because we don't possess this skill some of our relationships have been fractured due to financial stress. Some of us are unable to find a comfortable compromise when we and our mates don't have compatible money styles; some of us misuse or abuse commingled resources; and some of us don't think before we trust.

If money didn't touch every aspect of your life, if your relationship with money didn't reflect the relationship you have with yourself, and if how you and your mate handle money didn't expose what is and is not working in the relationship you two have together, there'd be no need for financial intimacy. But they do and there is.

I wrote *Financial Intimacy* for and about women in their thirties and forties, but not because we have special needs that are different from younger or older women or even from men. In fact, my twenty-three years in the financial services industry have given me the opportunity to work with women and men of all ages, and I know from firsthand experience that everyone, regardless of age or gender, is prone to making the same financial mistakes. Likewise, we all experience similar financial breakthroughs and successes. But unlike men, women oftentimes seem to suffer the negative consequences of money's duality to a far greater degree. And it pains me to see so many of the women in my generation (myself included) missing out on establishing deeper connections with our mates for reasons that can be mitigated.

Many women today earn significantly more than women in previous generations. But ironically that hasn't necessarily resulted in a higher degree of financial security. Some women adeptly handle the responsibilities that come with earning, saving, and investing more, but that doesn't mean their choices are always wise or that they possess financial confidence within the context of their relationships. Some women yearn to be strategic, realistic, and practical with their hearts and their purses, but wonder how to accomplish this when they haven't figured out how to deftly handle the questions money raises and the conflicts money will inevitably cause in their romantic relationships. Does any of this ring true for you?

From your quick trip down memory lane, you were probably reminded of an oft-overlooked financial truth: *money is never just about money.* The emotional component of money, which is shaped by your personal choices, experiences, family background, and interactions with society, is demanding and multidimensional, painfully so at times.

Here are a few more truths about money: If you want money to work for you, you not only have to be willing to work for it but also with it and on it. If you want money to work for you, you have to recognize that you don't really manage money, you manage choices. If you want money to work for you, you have to accept that there will always be an ongoing tension between your past, present, and future. But if you embrace this tension it can be your guide as you examine your thoughts on, beliefs about, and behavior with money. It can be the funnel through which you explore how you arrive at the financial choices you make, and how everything interrelates to affect one of your most intimate relationships—the one you have (or will have) with your mate.

I am on a mission to turn money into the unlikely tool that facilitates what couples learn about each other and how they grow together. As such, it is the goal of *Financial Intimacy* to put the many truths about money to work *for* you. Written as a combination of "how come" and "how to" for women of all marital statuses, straight or gay, this book is a modest attempt to elevate the conversations normally had between couples about money. Because, let's face it, if you're not able to have significant and substantive conversations about money, what else are you unable to discuss? What else are you unable to confront in your relationship? And if you reach a point where discussions about money are as painless as discussing what to eat for dinner, imagine what else you can accomplish in the way of communication.

In the process, I hope to satisfy your thirst for knowledge on how to manage money's emotional influence on your romantic relationship. Equally, I hope to inspire you to think about things you had not considered before, or to think differently about what you already do know. I hope to encourage you to engage in self-reflection and unfamiliar conversations so that you and your mate can expand your financial self-awareness and improve your fiscal fitness skills. And I hope to give you insight that will help you take the lead in fostering transparency on what is typically a sensitive and potentially precarious topic.

The book is divided into three sections, each reflecting a necessary and sequential ingredient for managing the intersection of love and money: understanding other people's stories, understanding your own story, and creating a framework for intimacy with your mate.

Other People's Stories

Vernon Law, former Pittsburgh Pirates pitcher, said during an interview, "Experience is the worst teacher; it gives the test before presenting the lesson." How true! Most people operate from the paradigm that experience is the best teacher. But learning from what others have or have not done is an excellent way to get the lesson without having to take the test! It can be just as insightful, but much less stressful. That is the purpose of this section.

I interviewed a broad spectrum of women for the seventeen real-life profiles you are about to read. Most of the women live on the East Coast; three live on the West. Each woman was asked the same set of questions, modified slightly to reflect her marital status and her sexual orientation. You will meet: Glenise, who is single and halfway through her list of one hundred things she wants in a partner; Leah, a part-time stay-at-home mother who sometimes feels self-conscious about her choice to partially opt out; Christine, a married mother of two and high-powered fashion executive with a stay-at-home husband, who remembers the days when she and her husband rolled quarters to buy milk; Mary Anne, who told her live-in boyfriend she had $44,000 in debt when it is actually $70,000; Miriam and Robin, a lesbian couple whose daughter inspired them to get their financial house in order; Jody, an assistant college provost who may have to make a one-time payment of six figures as part of her divorce settlement; and Toni, who while still in her forties has been single, married, widowed, engaged, and is now single again. Their stories, along with the others, will give you a peek into their lives, their choices, and their lessons.

All of the stories are deeply personal to the women interviewed, yet they reflect the financial and emotional challenges every woman, to some degree, eventually faces when the relationships she has with herself, her money, and her mate converge. As you read their stories, you'll read about the things that shape all of us: family background, personal choices, and socioeconomic and sociocultural influences. Interspersed throughout their stories are my interpretations of how the social changes of the last forty years have affected the fabric of our individual and collective lives.

Your Story

You use money every day, be it in the form of cash, debit/credit cards, or online transactions. Yet if you ask most people if they have a *relationship* with money, they'd look askance. Rarely does one associate the word *relationship* with money even though you have a long-standing relationship with it, one that was first formed when you were a child. But like any other relationship, our interaction with money is very personal, often conditional, and always central to our vision of the future.

At its genesis, your relationship with money is what got you the piece of candy you wanted from the corner store, the ice cream cone from the ice-cream truck, or the latest Happy Meal toy from McDonald's. Interestingly, early childhood is probably when you had the most authentic relationship with money; that is when you intuitively understood its true nature as a medium of exchange and as a means to a desirable end.

As you got older, though, you started to notice that the truth about money and the reality of how you experienced it were often quite different. While you probably didn't understand this duality, you certainly *felt* it every time you compared what you and your family had or didn't have relative to other people.

Eventually, money's functional purpose was overshadowed by the emotions you attached to it—both the feelings that were masked, as well as those that were revealed. This may have marked an inflection point in your relationship with money. You were just a teenager then, so while you were aware of money's importance, you had not fully grasped its meaning. However, what you knew for sure was that money measured more than the cost of the item you wanted to purchase.

Fast-forward twenty or thirty years. Life experiences have given you a little more clarity regarding the meaning of money, and it now feels more personal. It seems that every choice you make, from where you work, to what you buy, to how you invest, becomes an extension of your "identity." Each says something about who you are. For this, you can thank the daily barrage of messages—some of which you adopted, others you created— about what you should have, do, buy, and be. Your behavioral responses to these messages become the elements of your financial story.

Your story is nothing short of a personal narrative, designed to reveal details about your past, present, and anticipated future. It is what makes you *who* you are; likewise, your story provides the backdrop as to *why* you are the way you are.

You may have received formal training on how to manage your personal finances, but more than likely, everything you learned about what to do with your money came primarily from what you observed people of long-standing influence, such as your parents, doing and what verbal messages they gave you about money. Additional sources of your financial education include other relatives, friends, the media, your religious or spiritual beliefs, popular culture, and of course your own experiences. Behind each choice, whether conscious or subconscious, is a silent decision to copy or reject what you learned from your varied teachers.

Every choice you make adds to your financial story on a real-time basis, revealing whether you have a strong and healthy relationship with money, a weak and self-defeating one, or something in between. Just as all relationships are mirrors of what you love, like, and dislike, and just as all relationships are fluid and dynamic, so is the relationship you have with money. This section is dedicated to helping you discover what you may not already know you know about your own story, and to helping you reconnect with the important elements you may have forgotten about that mold your thoughts, behavior, and expectations concerning money.

You and Your Mate

Everything that is true about your personal narrative is also true in parallel for your mate. And when you get together with someone, you're dealing with your issues with money as well as his or hers! In the same way that you copy or reject what you learned to do with your money from various teachers, so has your mate. And typically, you either want your mate to imitate what you do with money or you want him or her to compensate for your behavior by doing the exact opposite.

Granted, not all relationships require financial intimacy to function, but financial intimacy does require a deep connectedness to exist. This section is intended to nurture that connectedness with the full understanding that there is no such thing as a one-size-fits-all solution and that, ultimately, financial intimacy will not look the same for every couple. It provides a framework for asking questions that will help you get to know what makes your mate's story his or her own. Likewise, it is intended to foster an exchange that will enable you to share what makes your story yours. In the process, you and your mate will tap into emotions you might not be accustomed to expressing. You will learn about each other's financial preferences, prejudices, and tolerances. And you will learn how to create a paradigm for living wealthy and well, in good times and bad.

You will also discover the silent expectations you impose on one another and what to do when these morph into emotional and financial blind spots (we all have them). Uncovering your respective blind spots is critical so that what you don't know doesn't sabotage your efforts to create financial intimacy.

The whole love-and-money dance begins with a series of questions that envelope the entire life cycle of the relationship. Questions are what got you this far, wherever that may be, and they are what will take you to the next level, whatever you want that to be.

I am asking you to pioneer a new landscape for yourself with little evidence to offer you that what we're doing is the right thing or that we are going about it in the right way. But we know that what we have been doing doesn't always work either—our relationships with money and our mates should be healthier. The emotional and financial stakes are too high to let financial intimacy continue to be absent from our lives. So while you might not know precisely where this journey will take you, it is time to start it nonetheless.

Financial Intimacy

1

Other People's Stories

"We make our world significant by the courage of our questions and by the depth of our answers."

—CARL SAGAN

Searching to Find the One

Glenise

There are 63 million single, never-married people in the United States, half of whom are women.[1] Why are there so many single women in the most industrialized country in the world, in the twenty-first century? Is this an unintended by-product of the civil rights and women's movements of the 1960s and 1970s? Is it because women today don't face the same economic pressures to marry as did the young women of our mothers' generation? Is it because, as some have said, a woman's career has replaced marriage as her number one goal? Is it because reproductive rights enable a woman to control when she gives birth and by extension enable her to delay marriage? Or is it because, even in a culture that places an emphasis on family, being a single woman no longer carries the social stigma it once did?

I'll leave it to the social psychologists to provide us with insight as to why the number of single, never-married women has doubled since 1977, when the number was approximately 16.5 million, or better yet, why the U.S. Department of Labor and Bureau of Labor Statistics include teenage boys and girls as young as sixteen years of age in the count. Nevertheless, the numbers can't hide the upward trend, a trajectory I find quite interesting when you take into account that more people are single today, either by choice or by default, even though the opportunities to date across races, cultures, and socioeconomic classes is greater and more socially acceptable.

Not only are there more single women today than in our mothers' generation, but also many are staying single well into their thirties and forties. This presents several challenges on the financial front. How do single women with fully developed financial identities and styles navigate the equally familiar and unfamiliar terrain called dating, especially if their ultimate aim is to merge their lives and finances (in some form) with partners?

Inspired by an article she recently read, Glenise has been steadily working on her list of one hundred things that she wants in a mate. You may have created such a list yourself, especially if you have ever read a self-help book espousing the benefits of writing down your goals, dreams, and desires. Such lists, in my opinion, are a great way of gathering information, first about yourself (what is important to you) and then about the other person (what attributes you are hoping the person you're dating or hoping to date will embody). Glenise is hoping—like many single women, including myself, who've put such lists together— that it will help her do a better job of separating the chaff from the wheat.

A month into this exercise, she is almost halfway done, and at the top of her list of what she's looking for in a partner, at numbers one and two, respectively, are *self-aware* and *self-made*. "Believe it or not," she says, "*self-made* for me does not mean financial although it does tie into that. [What] it really means is [someone who has had] some sense of struggle and not a life where everything was handed to [them] because I don't understand that." Given her life story, this isn't surprising.

Glenise's parents met in the early 1960s when her father was a student at Howard University. When she was six, the family relocated to Nigeria, his home country. Her father accepted a position with the Nigerian government, and they lived on Victoria Island in a tony housing complex built specifically for civil servants. By African standards Glenise's family was middle class; they lived in an affluent neighborhood, had servants, and took family vacations. Additionally, Glenise was sent to boarding school for five years. Yet she is quick to point out that, even with all these comforts of wealth, "money didn't feel abundant." As examples, she tells me about never having extra money while at boarding school and having to wear her uniforms until they almost fell apart.

She graduated from boarding school at fifteen, in June of 1986, and was scheduled to attend college in the coming fall. But this plan was thwarted when her parents (unexpectedly to her) separated. Soon after, Glenise, her younger sister, and her mother moved back to the United States. That move shifted their financial situation to the opposite end of the economic spectrum: poverty. They went from living a middle-class life-style to being on welfare and calling Section 8 public housing home. The welfare was temporary, but her mother still lives in the projects.

It is common knowledge that when a woman, especially one with children, separates or divorces, her standard of living is likely to drop significantly. Does it decrease by 73 percent as Dr. Lenore J. Weitzman claimed in her research? Her study influenced the law and the thinking of presidents, judges, commentators, and other sociologists. Or is it a much lower number? According to Dr. Richard R. Peterson, a sociologist who reevaluated Dr. Weitzman's findings, the number is closer to 27 percent.[2] For some, these are merely statistics; but for others, like Glenise, plummeting down the economic ladder was a reality she, her sister, and their mother lived.

Instead of going to college in September of 1986, Glenise started twelfth grade at a public high school in Baltimore, and in March of the following year, she started her first job. The plan was to get an American high school diploma, work to save money for college, and apply to American colleges. Little did she know this was the beginning of an eleven-year journey during which she'd work a bit, go to school a bit, and sometimes do both simultaneously. In that time, she was accepted into four colleges—her father's alma mater, Howard University; Florida A&M University (FAMU); Fashion Institute of Technology (FIT); and Smith College—deferred admission to two (Howard and FIT), attended two (FAMU and Smith), and graduated from one (Smith). By the time she entered Smith as a full-time, nontraditional student, she was twenty-four. By the time she finished, she was twenty-seven with a degree in African American studies, a lot of credit card and student loan debt, a more developed personal philosophy, and a naive understanding of the relationship between money and matters of the heart.

Back then, she was a self-described feminist. To her that translated into being a modern, independent woman who didn't subscribe to any traditional scripts about dating (she dates men and women) or any set rules about money in relationships. Today, Glenise is thirty-seven, single, almost debt-free, savvy about investing, and owns her apartment in New York City. And she has shifted her views slightly about how she wants the intersection of love and money to play out in her life. Gone are the days of no set rules, thanks in large part to age, wisdom, and a profound fear of being "old and broke."

Perhaps because of her own story, she has a history of connecting with people around their narratives (how they got to where they are). She finds this extremely attractive and ties into the self-made quality she's seeking. Though she cares about money, it is never the first thing she thinks about. In fact, more often than not, she's dated people who have earned less money than she does. We both laugh at the irony of this because she does nonprofit work and, as she says, "[I] should not be the one making the most money in any situation!"

She tells me of one date with a woman who only ordered an appetizer. Glenise kept wondering throughout their dinner, "Are you not hungry, or is that all you can afford?" But she didn't press the issue because she didn't want to offend her date, nor was she in a position to pay for both of them. She recounts another experience when she dismissed the fact that the guy she was dating made less than she did. Her rationale was "I'm a feminist, so that doesn't matter." In both cases, money was an issue not fully spoken about or addressed.

Possibly, the matter of who makes more or who has more disposable income wouldn't be too much of a concern if other things were in place. But what has typically accompanied these scenarios for Glenise is that the other person is also not financially stable. So on top of not matching her earnings, the other person's financial standing posed a potential risk to his or her well-being as well as hers. That's a rather unsettling notion for someone as industrious and self-determined as she is. She has worked very hard to create in her adult life what she didn't always have growing up: financial security, stability, and abundance.

Glenise remains interested in a person's narrative, but she's not willing to get involved with a person who doesn't have savings and a retirement plan, health insurance, manageable debt, disposable resources, and a generous spirit. In other words, she's looking for someone with similar financial priorities, aspirations, and habits. Her shift in perspective has been under way for several years, and her new thinking about money and dating and love is definitely much more mature than it was ten years ago. Actually, it goes hand-in-hand with getting older, growing wiser, and allowing money to take its rightful place in her romantic relationships.

Sabrina

I wanted the real-life case studies in this book to reflect a broad cross-section of women and their experiences. Likewise, I was committed to including profiles that represented all marital statuses (single, married, same-sex partnered, divorced, and widowed). To source interview candidates, I cast a wide net with just two requirements: each woman had to be college-educated and born in the 1960s or 1970s. Everything else, such as race, ethnicity, country of origin, family's socioeconomic background, and geographic location was purposely left open. In response to my query for interview prospects, more women responded than I could have ever imagined or in fact needed, and they were just as diverse as I wanted them to be, with one exception.

All the women who identified as single, never-married were black! This includes not just the women whose profiles are included in the book, but also those with whom I spoke and whose stories are not in these pages. This was perplexing to me, and initially I considered it a fluke and set out to get more prospects in hopes of rounding out this section. Then I learned that black women represent a significant portion of the approximately thirty million single, never-married women in America.

The Joint Center for Political and Economic Studies, using data sourced from the U.S. Census Bureau, reported that 81 percent of white women and 77 percent of Hispanic and Asian women will marry by age thirty, but only 52 percent of black women will marry by that age.[3] I didn't have to look too far for confirmation of these statistics. I'm forty-three and single, and I know a number of black women, personally and professionally, who are also single and older than thirty.

Marriage is a definite goal for many women, including me. Yet there is a distinct possibility that we may remain unmarried. In May 1999, Barbara Butrica, Lee Cohen, and Howard Iams, at the First Annual Joint Conference for the Retirement Research Consortium, presented a finding I found startling. In their presentation, "Introduction and Findings from the Model of Income in the Near Term (MINT) Project," they revealed that 18.6 percent of black, single, never-married women who were born between 1946 and 1964 (baby boomers) are projected to be unmarried at age sixty-two compared to 5.1 percent of the same population of women who were born between 1926 and 1930 (Depression era). If we assume the same growth pattern, the number of black Generation X and Millennial women who have never married by age sixty-two could potentially rise to 55.8 percent.

Numbers have a way of personalizing cold, hard facts and revealing possible truths that many of us may not be ready to digest. I don't share this information to be a doomsayer. But these statistics should remind single, never-married women in general, and single, never-married black women in particular, to avoid playing the waiting game. In other words, don't defer financial decisions, both small and large, in anticipation of marriage, because there is a strong possibility you may not marry. (Actually, it is unwise to defer financial decisions in general. You run the risk of missing out on the benefit that comes with time being on your side.) And furthermore, if you are looking to marry Prince Charming, he may never show up.

Women make financial decisions every day, ranging from the simple to the complex. So being financially self-reliant and self-dependent is not new for many women, especially black women. What is new, however, are the perceived societal expectations of college-educated, professional women born in the 1960s and '70s. "Earlier generations of college-educated women picked either work or family, work after family, or family after work; those [like us] who graduated [undergrad and grad school] in the 1980s and 1990s are the first to be expected to do both at the same time," writes E. J. Graff in the essay "The Opt-Out Myth."[4] As such, our generation is probably the first for whom, given our credentials, the expectation is that we shouldn't need or want Prince Charming to show up.

Who is Prince Charming, beyond the fictional character who saves the damsel in distress in all the fairy tales? For the purposes of this book, I define him as someone who has positive and ever-increasing earning power and potential, is financially responsible and able to take care of you, and someone upon whom you can and do financially rely and depend.

Sabrina, an entertainment attorney in private practice, is financially savvy, self-reliant, and self-dependent. During our interview she admitted for the first time, "I'm looking for someone who I feel is my Prince Charming." It wasn't necessarily a newfound awareness for her, but it was the first time she gave herself permission to say it aloud. "I'm a little bit more traditional . . . so, I'd lean towards saying I'd want him to [earn] more than me, take care of our family, and be financially responsible," she says.

At thirty-eight, she's lost a bit of the naivete she once had about a relationship being able to survive on love alone and money not making a difference. She is looking to break a pattern of dating men who were phenomenal people but "who were very free-flowing, a little too free-flowing [for her taste] with money." One guy was an artist who literally had no money. They ended up spending most of their time together at home instead of going out. Another was an attorney with a salary on par with hers but whose carefree spending raised a red flag. In an interesting twist of fate, with him she'd have preferred if they ate in once in a while. Whether they earned a little or a lot, ironically, most of the men she's dated, including her long-term relation-ships, were men who were the exact opposite of her father in terms of financial prowess.

Sabrina's parents divorced when she was eight. After the divorce, her father won full custodial rights of Sabrina and her younger siblings. (Fathers winning custody and becoming the primary caregivers for their children due to divorce may not be unusual in 2009, but it was atypical in the 1970s.) This would be the first of many precedents set by her father, a police offi-cer who quickly rose through the ranks and is now the chief of housing police in the large metropolitan city where Sabrina grew up and currently lives.

Many other precedents would follow, including the lifestyle he provided for his family, which eventually expanded to include a longtime girlfriend and another child. What Sabrina remem-bers is a sense of being taken care of; she says, "We weren't rich, but we lived pretty well." Her father took care of everything, and though he made each of his children get part-time jobs in high school, it wasn't because he couldn't afford to give them an allow-ance. He simply wanted them to develop a strong work ethic.

Sabrina describes her father as a strict disciplinarian, a finan-cial caregiver, and someone who is "meticulous with money." None of this, however, translated into him teaching her about what she should do with money or how. An example she shares is the credit card trouble she got into during college. "When I went to college, I remember distinctly [being] one of those kids who opened a credit card and went crazy racking up a lot of debt. My father swooped in and paid it off and then chastised me." Even today, her father will help any of his children if they ask him for financial help but only after he asks them, "What are you going to do with the money? What do you need it for, and why can't you work for it?" In the end, he always gives them the money they need.

While she has always had the comfort and security of know-ing she could rely on her father if necessary, Sabrina set out to learn about money on her own. As a result, she can now include herself in the group of financially savvy women: she invests in the stock market, owns her apartment, owns a business, is now a disciplined saver, and uses credit card debt strategically. And she does something else that isn't directly tied to money management but is crucial to one's financial health nonetheless: she surrounds herself with friends who have similar financial habits. Clearly, she's not playing the waiting game. If she gets married (and I hope she does), she'll be coming to the proverbial table with financial assets and healthy habits.

Couple the work she's done on her own to amass her wealth and develop sound financial practices with her experiences growing up and dating, and it isn't too much of a surprise that she has evolved from feeling money doesn't matter to embracing that it does. Why would she want to jeopardize the financial security she has worked so hard to establish? For her, this means marrying Prince Charming. And this brings me to two issues I believe are missing from the Prince Charming debate. The first is that the focus is usually on how much Prince Charming earns without taking into account if he is a good financial steward. It's just as dangerous to presume a high earner is also proficient with managing money as it is to presume someone with a modest income, perhaps due to his chosen profession, is not. The second issue is that being with someone who is financially irresponsible is equally hazardous as abdicating complete control. In my opinion, the debate needs to expand; for far too long it has been narrowly confined to a discourse about financial independence and dependence, but has left out the possibility of finding a way to be interdependent.

Even if most conversations about Prince Charming are hush-hush, it is important to talk about him since the myth and reality of him is just as bona fide today as it has been in past generations, and the number of women who may remain unmarried is rising. The benefit of talking about him is that it helps you decide, define, and prepare: decide if you really want a Prince Charming; define what that actually means to you and for you; and prepare yourself financially, as well as perhaps emotionally, for the possibility that marriage may not happen and he might not appear. In this way, you can figure out, at least financially, how to be your own Princess Charming.

Patrice

I am writing this book at a particular historical moment in the United States that bodes very well for the conversations I hope to spark. Clearly I could not have orchestrated the coincidence of either the timing of the economic and political events that are making 2009 a hallmark year thus far or the events themselves, but I am grateful for the unplanned concatenation.

Today the economy is the midst of the deepest recession since the Depression era. The defining line between an "unofficial" (read: what people experience) and "official" recession was crossed during the summer of 2008 when we had two consecutive quarters of negative economic growth—the official definition of a recession. Some would argue that the current recession began late in 2007.

The unemployment rate, value of homes, and gross domestic product (GDP) or the output of goods and services produced are but a few of the ways to assess the health of the economy. You hear about these and other factors all the time, but what typically dominates the evening news is the performance of the stock market and the price of crude oil. As I write, the ever-fluctuating stock market as measured by the Dow Jones Industrial Average is in bear territory. Not only is it down from the peak reached in October 2007, it is at a level not seen since February 1997, the first time it closed above seven thousand points. Last summer the price of crude oil was trading above $146 a barrel, an unprecedented high. Currently, it is trading at $48.14. To put this number into perspective and to prove why oil trading above $100 is uncharacteristic: the inflation-adjusted price per barrel during the 1973 oil crisis was $40! What the recession and the alternating inverse and converse relationship between the price of oil and the price of stocks mean for those of us who are "average" investors—meaning we didn't speculate on the oil industry or migrate our portfolios to cash to lock in our previous gains before the start of the recession—is that our portfolios are down, significantly.

Pundits describe the current economic and investing environment as the "credit crunch." What people are feeling is a financial crunch, and they are feeling it in many areas of their lives, not just with regard to their investment portfolios (presuming of course, they have them). Simply put, it is costing more to live your day-to-day life in 2009 than it did just a year ago. That's the bad news. But "bad" news, in general, and "bad" financial news, in particular, always force people to pay attention to things that seem immaterial when everything—like the economy or a good-paying job—is going well and momentum is pulling you forward rather than a strategy.

Something else forcing people to take notice is the election of a black man, Barack Obama, as the president of the United States. When you consider that forty years ago black people in America's South couldn't vote and lived within a racial caste system, this is a tremendous milestone.

I cannot hide my personal excitement about President Obama's election and what it connotes about our country's growth. But I am also excited about his administration for another reason: it is serving as a catalyst for a conversation regarding the needs, struggles, and desires of black, college-educated, professional women. When the media covers his wife, Michelle Obama, whether the coverage is deemed positive or negative, a spotlight is cast on issues that are important to all women, yet experienced by black women in ways unique to us despite the educational and socioeconomic diversity within our race. Our individual and collective issues are not drastically different from those of other women, but the social context of our history definitely is.

The history of black women in America is complex and multifarious, and many facets of our lives are rarely looked at comprehensively outside of African American women's studies programs in academia. And there is one aspect that gets minimal attention in academia and even less consideration in other arenas: the challenges and victories of black women managing the intersection of love and money. Even *NBC Nightly News with Brian Williams*, which ran a five-part series entitled "African-American Women: Where They Stand" in November 2007 and covered topics such as education, marriage and family structures, interracial dating, health, and the role of black women in politics, didn't delve into this two-prong relationship.

Coverage of the First Lady and other black women in the Obama administration can do what commercial television and traditional media outlets heretofore have not: shed light on why young black women of the 1960s and '70s (our parents) experienced the women's movement—whether they were actively involved or not—differently than their Hispanic, Asian, and, especially, white counterparts, and why the same still holds true for their offspring in the twenty-first century. This coverage provides an opportunity to start a national debate about a topic that rarely gets discussed on a national platform. In the process, a broader audience can be engaged in the conversation about the needs, struggles, and desires of black women, in general, and the college-educated, professional subset, in particular, thereby offering "outsiders" a peek into a world relatively unknown to them. Likewise, "insiders" can receive confirmation that they are not alone. And finally, this coverage can provide an opportunity to begin a forthright conversation as to why the majority of black women can't talk about managing love and money without including another element: work.

As Raina Kelly notes in her *Newsweek* article about Michelle Obama, "A Real Wife, In a Real Marriage," "Black women have never been burdened with the luxury of choice. Our heritage does not include the gilded cage, and we certainly never fought to labor outside the home—black women have always worked." And because many, if not all, of the women in our families have always worked and, subsequently, so have my peers and I, we don't consider the increasing numbers of dual-income households or women earning more than their husbands as trailblazing trends. These have simply been realities for many black women for decades.

Imagine being able to trace your family's roots back to the late 1800s; imagine continuing today a family legacy begun 118 years ago. When Patrice graduated from New York University, she became the fourth generation of women on the maternal side of her family to complete college. When she started her boutique sports and entertainment public relations firm ten years ago, she was following in the entrepreneurial footsteps of her great-grandmother who was born in the late 1800s, graduated college, became a nurse, and started a home-care nursing service for "very wealthy [white] people in Virginia." Quite a remarkable achievement given that she was born just one generation post slavery!

The elders in Patrice's family often remark about the similarities between her and her great-grandmother. They seem to see in Patrice her great-grandmother's personality, self-determination, and financial prowess. And of this, she is proud. In many ways, by emulating her great-grandmother (even if it is unintentional), she is paying homage to her living family members who made sure to pass down the values of the family's progenitors. But when it comes to dating (and potentially marrying), she doesn't envision being able to do for the children she hopes to have what her parents did for her and her brother, if she follows in her great-grandmother's footsteps and marries a man who is not her peer educationally and professionally.

To describe Patrice's great-grandmother as a progressive woman is probably an understatement. In spite of the times in which she lived, she made great strides educationally and professionally. Who she married was also a sign of the times in which she lived. She married a school custodian. In the early twentieth century, Patrice's great-grandmother was part of a dual-income household and was the primary earner. Today, there's every possibility that Patrice will also be part of a dual-income household and potentially the primary earner. But as a sign of her times, she desires to marry someone who is her educational and professional peer. We don't know if this is something her great-grandmother desired as well; we do know that one generation post slavery, her options to do so were severely limited.

Black, college-educated, professional women have been marrying blue-collar men for a very, very long time. Doing so today, however, seems to cause a number of women who were born in the 1960s or '70s a great deal of angst. If you listen to women of earlier generations, they didn't feel their union with blue-collar men was an unequal paring. Whereas women in their thirties and forties today see disparity, their mothers, grandmothers, and great-grandmothers saw themselves and their husbands each doing what was necessary to provide for their families. Perhaps the difference is in how we define *professional*. *Professional* back then pretty much meant you were a nurse, educator, or social worker. Today its meaning is much, much broader and extends beyond the aforementioned professions to include lawyers, doctors, investment bankers, politicians, and business owners.

Patrice's father holds a master's degree in chemistry and worked for a chemical company in executive management until he retired. Her mother holds a master's degree in early childhood development and works as an educator. Both her parents worked hard to provide for her and her brother a "rich" childhood, not in a financial sense but experientially. The family traveled extensively within the United States as well as internationally. She and her brother participated in an array of extracurricular activities, like ballet, horseback riding, and summer camps, and they both graduated from college debt free. Patrice wants to do what almost every parent or parent-to-be aspires to do: give her offspring the same as she had at a minimum, or more if possible.

She has never had the expectation that a man will take care of her, but Patrice is looking for "someone [who] could come to the table with at least what [she is] bringing to the table." The revenue from the public relations firm she launched in 1999 has fluctuated from nothing to in excess of $250,000 in some years. She also earns a salary from an adjunct professor position she took on a few years ago. She has a sizeable investment portfolio (at one point, a single holding in her portfolio was valued at $150,000), and she owns both her primary residence and investment property. She's been saving since her very first job, at eleven years of age. She worked at the church's nursery as a babysitter and would deposit every check in a savings account her father opened for her—and she rarely made withdrawals.

All of the men with whom she's had serious relationships, including her ex-fiancé, were college-educated and professional. Education is a nonnegotiable requirement of hers. As shared earlier, she's the fourth generation of women on her maternal side to graduate college. Her brother is the third generation of men in the family to graduate college on their maternal side, and second on their paternal side. It is very important to Patrice to continue this legacy of education.

And though they've all been professional, she's dated men who earned significantly less than her as well as considerably more. From the former, she's learned to be vague about what she does—owning a sports and entertainment public relations agency has been downshifted to "consulting." She doesn't share that she owns a home or a car, never mind that she drives a ten-year-old Jeep. She didn't like the reactions when she disclosed these aspects of her life. In one instance, the guy said, "What do you need me for?" When she replied, "To share a life," he looked at her askance. From the men who earned more than she does, she learned that just because someone has financial resources it doesn't necessarily mean they make smart financial decisions. Her ex-fiancé, for example, happened to earn considerably more than she did, but didn't share her financial philosophy. For example, he bought a house with a mortgage 35 percent more than his current mortgage, which was already a stretch. That didn't make sense to Patrice. He bought a new luxury car when the one he had was working fine. When he launched his law practice (he is an entertainment attorney), he moved into a posh office and hired a full-time assistant. Patrice felt a less fancy office space and a part-time assistant would have been a better use of his investment capital until the business really got up and running.

Her ex-fiancé had the resources but lacked the habits and discipline she's been practicing since she was an eleven-year-old child. The men she out-earned lacked a sense of self-comfort and were unable to get beyond her tremendous earning power in comparison to theirs. (I believe this is worse than not having equal resources.) Neither type of man would be able to help Patrice with her goal of providing for her future children what her parents had provided for her and her brother.

No, a college-educated, professional man doesn't come with a guarantee of financial compatibility—you won't automatically end up with someone who shares the same financial habits and philosophy as you. But to see in Patrice's story only a blue-collar versus white-collar trade-off is far too simplistic a posture to take. It omits the need and desire we each have to be with someone who mirrors our goals and aspirations, and discounts the internal struggle we experience when we don't want a man who might be like our uneducated, nonprofessional father, grandfather, or great-grandfather—even though without them, in most instances anyway, we wouldn't be where we are today, ourselves college-educated and professional.

The women's issue that gets the most media attention today can best be summed up in a sentence penned by Raina Kelly in the same *Newsweek* article referenced earlier: "Many of us never inherited the remorse about balancing work and family that plagues our white counterparts." The "many of us" to which she is referring are black women. No, many of us don't have the remorse she describes; ours is a different kind of remorse, which comes from rejecting a part of our history in an effort to create our future. This struggle doesn't get any media attention.

But it could, inadvertently. As Mrs. Obama travels the country in her role as First Lady, she reminds us that "women's issues" isn't a homogeneous term; it means something different to everyone and has different consequences for us all. Likewise, coverage of her helps to broaden the definition and understanding of what it means to be a woman managing the intersection of love, money, and work.

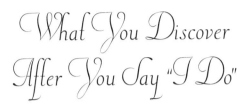

What You Discover
After You Say "I Do"

Delissa

For selfish reasons, I purposely set out to interview people I didn't know at all or very well—I thought it'd be more interesting to learn about the stories of strangers. Plus, I feared that with the interviewees I knew, we could potentially lapse, due to our familiarity, into a zone of presuming a certain level of knowledge about intimate details that may or may not be accurate.

Given our friendship of more than ten years and the fact that I was one of her bridesmaids, Delissa didn't meet my interviewee criteria. Yet a casual conversation about how my research and writing were coming along led to a revelation that prompted me to reconsider. It just so happened that we were talking a week before Delissa and Elia's one-year wedding anniversary.

Delissa is black; Elia is white. She's American; he's European, Swiss-German to be exact. They are a stunning couple. Looking at them, I'm reminded of one of my favorite movies, *Paris Blues*, which is kind of funny because she's an actress and he's a cinematographer, and they are both jazz enthusiasts.

Made in 1961 and starring Paul Newman, Sidney Poitier, Diahann Carroll, and Joanne Woodward, *Paris Blues* was, in my opinion, way ahead of its time, on the verge of being scandalous. If you read a synopsis of the movie, it will definitely talk about two jazz musicians (Mr. Newman and Mr. Poitier's characters) living in Paris, where jazz is appreciated and racism is not. It will definitely talk about how they meet and fall in love with two American women (Ms. Carroll and Ms. Woodward's characters). But something you would know only from seeing the movie is that Newman's character initially falls for Carroll's character! The attraction was short-lived—interracial love, even on-screen, was mostly untouchable then, at the height of America's civil rights movement.

Forty years ago Delissa and Elia's marriage would have been illegal in most states in America. I was two years old when the U.S. Supreme Court struck down the last remaining anti-miscegenation law in 1967. Since then, the number of racial inter-marriages has steadily increased. In 1980, about 2 percent of mar-riages were interracial; by 2000, about 5.4 percent were interracial.[5] The upward trend in racial intermarriages has continued into the first part of the twenty-first century.[6] Census data showed 117,000 black wife/white husband couples in 2006, up from 95,000 in 2000. There were just 26,000 such couples in 1960.[7]

That she's black and he's white is an obvious, tangible differ-ence. Their financial differences, which were much less evident, came to light as they were planning their wedding. According to the Bridal Association of America, the average cost of a wed-ding in 2005 was $26,450; it's projected to cost $30,860 in 2009. By comparison, Delissa and Elia had a reasonable affair cost-ing a little over $20,000. In his mind, a wedding should cost about $4,000. (We don't know where he got that number, but it seemed sensible to him; $20,000 did not.)

Cost, however, wasn't the only issue Elia was grappling with. He doesn't believe in debt beyond a mortgage and couldn't understand putting so much money on a credit card. Delissa's reassurances that they'd pay it off by the end of the year brought him little comfort. Each time a new wedding-related charge appeared on the credit card statement, Elia would become so flabbergasted he'd "suddenly forget how to speak English and revert to his native German language."

It is not unusual to discover that you and your mate have dissimilar financial habits and beliefs. What is odd is that Del-issa and Elia would make this discovery after living together for four years and running a business together for three! Given that their financial lives were already entwined, one would assume this would already be known. Ironically, neither the process of buying a home nor the stress of launching a new business led to their fights about money—it was a $20,000 wedding, paid by credit card!

Credit cards originated in the United States in the 1930s, and their use became more widespread by the 1950s. Our use of credit cards is so pervasive that we lead the world in credit card circulation. *Frontline*, a PBS program, reported in the 2004 program "Secret History of the Credit Card" that the United States had nearly 1.3 billion credit cards in circulation; compare that to the next largest market, the United Kingdom, which had 59 million at the end of 2003. Americans' credit card usage is unparalleled—and so is our tolerance for debt. Total U.S. consumer debt, which includes installment debt, but not mortgage debt, reached $2.4 trillion in June 2007, up from $358 billion in 1968.[8] And it seems to be growing in lockstep with our nation's debt. Currently, the U.S. national debt is hovering around $11 trillion.

Delissa, her sister, and her brother were raised by their grandmother and her third husband. As Delissa describes growing up in a New Jersey suburb, she says, "We were not rich, but well off, better than the . . . black kids that I grew up around. We had a lot of property, a nice, big house, and we never wanted for anything. Plus, my brother, sister, and I went to private schools. And we had pretty much carte blanche at the stores [where] my grandmother carried credit."

She goes on to say, "My grandmother wasn't demonstrative in her affection, but she would always say, 'I don't show my love for you by coddling you. I show you by what I do for you and education is one way and what I buy for you [is another].'" Because her grandmother expressed her love for her grandchildren in large part via material things, Delissa learned to equate things with love and love with money. In addition, she came to expect that her every whim would be satisfied, because her grandmother never told her and her siblings no, nor did they ever suffer any consequences for misusing the accounts where she had credit. Delissa learned to freely spend money, but she was never given any guidance on how to manage it.

When Elia was two years old, his parents divorced. For several years following the divorce, his mother had a hard time financially. Six years later, Elia and his mother's financial picture changed drastically when she met and settled down with a "very wealthy guy." Though grateful for the opportunities his stepfather's wealth afforded him, like coming to the United States for college, Elia never fully embraced that he and his mother no longer had to struggle. He was hypervigilant about money. Interestingly, while he learned to be strategic about debt, he, too, was never given any guidance on how to manage money.

My interview with Delissa is one of the few I conducted in person. We met at Bar Sepia, the business she and Elia own. Their business is the epitome of the adages "timing is everything" and "location, location, location." Bar Sepia opened just before what has become known as "Brooklyn's boom"—referred to by us long-time residents as skyrocketing rental rates and unprecedented co-op/condo/brownstone sales—got under way. It is located in the Prospect Heights section of Brooklyn (the new hot area), a few short blocks from the acclaimed Brooklyn Museum of Art. Though the business is operating in the black, it, like any business, has had its share of ups and downs—including the common challenge of staff turnover. She had a new bartender in training that night, which is why we were meeting there. The low-playing music, background chatter from the patrons, and a few interruptions from the bartender couldn't dim, however, what was becoming clearer the longer we talked: emotions are always rational after the fact.

The likelihood that you will end up with someone whose family's experiences with money are akin to yours is slim to none. Yet these experiences shape much of how you perceive the role of money in your life and influence the degree to which you are financially astute and responsible. It is easy to see how Delissa would be comfortable paying for the wedding using a credit card. She grew up in a debt-friendly country and in a household that encouraged her to use credit to buy whatever she wanted. This approach absolutely terrified Elia, who grew up with the understanding that you don't carry nonmortgage debt, and you pay your bills in full as they come in.

They knew these details about each other, plus some. For example, Delissa has a tendency to pay her bills late, even though she has the resources to pay them. On the flip side, Elia can be "penny wise and pound foolish" when it comes to protecting his assets. Until recently, he didn't have health and life insurance, not because he couldn't afford it but because he thought it wasn't a wise use of money for someone whose income was good yet sporadic. He rationalized it by asking, "What if I don't get sick? What if I don't die?" However, knowing each other's history and current pattern and where you differ is one thing. Understanding what triggers a reaction to those differences is quite another. It is this mysterious variable that leads to fights, especially about money.

Money management skills involve much more than spending within your means, paying on time, or being prudent about debt. Competencies in these areas, though absolutely necessary, only represent part of the picture. Yet you'd never know this based on the way in which the term "manage money" is often bantered about. It is as if the act of managing money involves doing one singularly defined thing well and has a universal definition. Which is why I always remind people that you aren't really managing money, you are managing choices!

On the surface, one might assume Delissa and Elia were really fighting about a $20,000 debt. In actuality, theirs is the classic case of the visionary risk-taker attracting the practical, cautious one. A choice they've made to ensure that this difference works in their favor more times than it doesn't is to segment who pays for what (he handles the household bills; she the business bills). And they've agreed not to purchase big-ticket items unless they are both in agreement on the method by which they will be paid.

And yes, the wedding was paid off within a year.

Elizabeth

A friend of mine recently took her five-year-old son to the Museum of Modern Art in New York City. They were just about to exit the exhibit when he asked, "Mommy, what's that?" He was pointing to a typewriter. In that moment, my friend, who is in her late thirties, realized that her son had never seen one, so accustomed to using a computer all his (young!) life. We chuckled heartily as she retold the story because we both remembered our undergrad days when we wrote our term papers using typewriters and word processors. Today, we can essentially carry our computers in the palms of our hands. My, how times have changed.

Technology has certainly changed in the last forty years, evolving by leaps and bounds in the last twenty. In the same time frame, the structure of American families has changed just as drastically, redefining family living along the way.

It seems whenever we discuss the structure of family life, a comparison is made to the 1950s classic television show *The Adventures of Ozzie and Harriet*. The show, which featured real-life husband and wife, Ozzie and Harriet Nelson, and their children, David and Rick, typified the "traditional family" with "traditional roles." The father is the breadwinner, and the mother is a stay-at-home mother responsible for taking care of the children and household.

Though frequently criticized for not reflecting anything close to a real-life, typical family, *Ozzie and Harriet* is often the benchmark by which modern American society defines "family," and it is the model the government has and continues to use even today to set many of the financial policies that govern our lives. And so, you either had an *Ozzie and Harriet* upbringing or you didn't. I didn't.

Growing up, it appeared everyone except me had the *Ozzie and Harriet* household. My mother legally separated from my father when I was two. With this choice, my mother and I joined the ranks of family households maintained by women (with no spouse present), which rose from 3.6 million in 1950 to 5.5 million in 1970.[9] According to the U.S. Census Bureau, this figure had risen to 29.2 million households by 1996. I was twelve when my parents officially divorced in 1977, a year when divorce was still uncommon but beginning to be met with less disapproval. For proof, consider these statistics: In 1968, there were 584,000 divorces; the number had increased to over 1 million by 1979.[10]

My mother and Elizabeth's mother represent a few of the faces behind these divorce statistics. Whether by choice or by default, they were on the forefront of the change in family compositions and belonged to a growing club: divorced women raising children. Elizabeth's father left her mother and their seven children, one of whom has special needs, to enter the priesthood. Until this point, her father had been the breadwinner, and her mother had stayed at home. His departure was felt immediately on many levels, especially financially. The family would soon discover that his vow of poverty wasn't just his own. The family's socioeconomic status quickly went from lower-middle class to just above the poverty line.

Her mother became the sole breadwinner for the family, but her income at times wasn't enough to keep them from subsisting on food and clothing provided by the generosity of strangers and churches. She recalls numerous occasions when bags of groceries were "found" on their porch. They also moved a lot, always to a tougher neighborhood, it seemed.

Elizabeth's mother may not have been in a position to raise her seven children in the nicest of neighborhoods or give them a lot of material things, but she was determined that each of them would receive a great high school education. "Even though we lived in tough neighborhoods, my mom always researched which of the public schools were the best—especially for my sister with special needs—and made sure we attended those schools," says Elizabeth. It was at one such school that Elizabeth discovered her passion and talent for theater and met a teacher who encouraged her to go to college to study acting. But a career as an actress? To her, the idea was absurd. "To go into acting and to become an artist in a family like mine . . . was not at all practical. I mean, how would I put food on the table?" Such were the considerations of a then-seventeen-year-old!

Today, acting is exactly what Elizabeth does, and you've probably seen one of the movies or plays in which she has appeared—which is why we are not using her real name. Her husband, David (also not his real name), is also a performing artist. Elizabeth and David are not megastars whose images grace the front pages of magazines like *People* or *Us Weekly*, but they also are not starving artists. Thankfully, putting food on the table isn't a concern. Instead, what has kept Elizabeth up at night lately is an issue commonly faced by people who have spent many years paying down their debt. Once they've sent in their final payment and the balance is zero, the question becomes, "Now what?" This is the point Elizabeth is at, and during our interview it becomes clear that the "now what?" question comes up frequently for her and David. It is significant for reasons far beyond what to do with the extra $1,000 she now has each month.

The financial roles and rules of marriage have changed considerably in the last fifty years. If the *Ozzie and Harriet* prototype characterized the 1950s and an upsurge in divorces characterized the 1960s and 1970s, then the late 1980s and beyond can best be characterized by an increase in the growth of dual-income households. According to a Bureau of Labor Statistics report, there were approximately 17 million dual-earners in 1967. This number almost doubled by 2005, the latest year for which figures are available, to 29 million.[11] Fueling this latest shift is a combination of factors, including the economic necessity of needing more money to run a household, along with more women obtaining college and advanced degrees and correspondingly pursuing career opportunities, climbing the corporate ladder, and starting their own businesses.

Elizabeth says she didn't feel poor until she reached high school. She was surprised to learn that some of her classmates had televisions in their bedrooms, had cars, or had parents who bought them things. Unlike Elizabeth's family, David's family is upper-middle class. Both his parents are highly educated; his father is a successful entrepreneur, and his mother works as a senior executive with a nonprofit organization. But like Elizabeth, David grew up in a single-parent household—his parents divorced when he was a teenager. Neither of them has seen firsthand how two people negotiate individual and joint goals, needs, and wants—and money—where the end result is not divorce but a healthy marriage.

Elizabeth and David have been together for ten years, married for five. When they met, they discovered that they hailed from the same area of upstate New York, shared a mutual love for the entertainment industry, and had a similar financial challenge: a lot of debt. Despite being debt-laden and broke, as many people are when starting out in their careers, David paid for everything when he and Elizabeth went out. That changed six months into their relationship when he learned, through a friend of hers, that she actually made more money than he did. His expectation was that she should pay for herself since she earned more; clearly, by way of behavior, Elizabeth's expectation was different. This caused a lot of friction between them and was the genesis of their first fight about money.

"Yes," she says, "I am self-reliant and self-sufficient, but I wanted to feel coddled, and having my man pay for everything was one way of feeling pampered." So initially Elizabeth took to giving him money at the beginning of a date to balance the disparity between his sense of fairness and her desire to be taken care of. This worked for a while—Elizabeth still got to feel taken care of in a manner that was important to her—but soon they realized that this "fix" wasn't really working. It wasn't addressing Elizabeth's internal conflict about what it meant to be taken care of, nor did it acknowledge that David spoiled her in other ways, just not monetarily. Thus began a rocky period, and the first time the question "now what?" was raised.

On more than one occasion, money opened a few emotional land mines that took them by surprise. These instances always happened when they were both working multiple gigs between acting assignments—in other words, when they were feeling the financial stresses of a profession that can be cyclical and unpredictable. Once David even went so far as to suggest to Elizabeth, "Maybe you need to date an investment banker." At another time, after they were married, he told her she needed to earn more money when she was concerned about being able to pay her portion of the rent. For different reasons, both comments hit a raw nerve with Elizabeth, and each time another "now what?" conversation got under way.

Naturally, all this feels very personal to Elizabeth. In truth, she is really one woman among many who finds herself struggling with how to define "being taken care of" and how to measure it. Compared to previous generations, Elizabeth and many of her peers who are part of dual-income households have more financial control and input. Yet, they have no clue as to how to best manage this influence to get their needs for emotional and financial security met.

Elizabeth and David's career choices made it fairly certain that their relationship, and subsequently their marriage, would be "modern," but they had not considered exactly what that meant in terms of financial roles, responsibilities, and expectations. Says Elizabeth, "The elements in our lives, such as who's making more money at any given time and how much, change constantly. Neither of us ever really knows what we'll earn exactly [year to year]."

Even so, like most dual-career couples today, they have more disposable income than their parents could have ever imagined at their same age. Likewise, they are also dealing with higher and more expenses than their parents had. Most dual-earners, who in 2009 are in their thirties and forties, are navigating a terrain unfamiliar to them. They don't have a comparable model to follow, either in terms of what to do or what not to do.

Such is the case with Elizabeth and David. Through trial and error, they are working on creating their own model. For instance, they hold separate checking and savings accounts and go dutch on everything—household expenses, entertainment, vacations. Unless one of them is treating the other, they operate with the presumption that they are splitting the cost of whatever activity they are doing together. And if one of them wants to do something and the other says, "I can't afford to do that right now," the one with money can either offer to treat the other or go alone. They even distribute household work: he cooks, she cleans. They do this not because of how they saw their parents negotiate such matters but because it seems the most logical and practical arrangement for them right now.

The nature of their relationship and their respective liveli-hoods fosters a continuous dialogue about money and how it shows up in their relationship. As such, they constantly renego-tiate previously agreed upon arrangements. When I met Eliza-beth, she was celebrating six months of being debt-free. For the first time ever, she was contemplating investing—something she had always wanted to do but didn't feel she had the extra money to do. David has been debt-free for a few years and investing regularly in an individual retirement account.

The "now what?" question first raised ten years ago when David learned she earned more than him (at the time) became the foundation for a practice that continues today: frank, often brutally honest conversations about money. Emotions have run high, feelings have been hurt, and tears have flowed; but that hasn't stopped Elizabeth and David from traveling down a path that, to their knowledge, their parents did not venture. And today's "now what?" has them contemplating, for the first time ever, the possibility of pooling some money and opening a joint investment account.

Leah

In 2003, Lisa Belkin set off a firestorm with her *New York Times Sunday Magazine* article, "The Opt-Out Revolution." As has become her signature, Ms. Belkin writes about the intersection of life and work, and with this particular piece, she reignited what seems to be a never-ending debate about motherhood, choices, and work.

Her article chronicles eight women, all graduates of Princ-eton, who have chosen to opt out—the term used to describe some twenty-first-century college-educated professional wom-en's choice to stay home. In so doing she juxtaposes the choices fought for by Second Wave feminists with the choices exercised by women of the Third Wave generation. I recently reread the article and noticed I had the same reaction to it as I did when I initially read it five years ago: my generation has been hood-winked, even if not intentionally.

"You can have it all." This may not have been an explicit message of the women's movement, but it was definitely one of the takeaway messages I heard, thanks more to the commercialization of the Second Wave than anything else. Do you remember the Enjoli commercial? "I can bring home the bacon, fry it up in the pan, and never let you forget you're the man." From conversations with other women born in the 1960s and '70s, it is clear I was not alone in this understanding. What I and many of my peers have come to realize is that you *can't* have it all—at least not all at the same time.

As we have discovered, much of life is an imperfect balancing act filled with personal and professional tradeoffs that are inevitable and constant. In becoming reacquainted with the stories of the women Ms. Belkin profiles, I was reminded of a question I've been pondering for some time: how do personal choices morph into a collective social movement and debate, and then become the benchmark against which those personal choices are measured?

I realize it is perhaps unfair to narrowly characterize the missions of the Second Wave as the right to work and the Third Wave as the right to stay home. But when you look at the typical banter about and between these movements, these simplistic generalizations don't seem too far off the mark. Yet, when I listen to the inner struggles of women in their thirties and forties as they recount the financial and career ramifications of their choices, I can't help but wonder: where's the movement for the right to do what's right for you and your family?

A combination of circumstances and personal preference prevent Leah from opting out completely. She works as a branding and design consultant working with retailers on concept design and the development of their stores. She traded in working eighty-five-hour weeks, at a minimum, for eighty-hour months, a move she jokingly refers to as being "downwardly mobile."

Leah may no longer earn a six-figure salary or work for a large corporation, but given her frame of reference of women who juggle marriage, motherhood, and a career, the notion of not working has never occurred to her. Her grandmother and her mother were highly recognized physical therapists known for their use of the Alexander Technique, a body positioning, reeducation, and coordination technique that uses physical and psychological principles. It originated in England, and her grandmother was one of the first physical therapists to introduce it to the United States. Her mother, in particular, became well-known for using it as a form of physical therapy for people with scoliosis. Her father, who is a writer and lecturer, is also highly regarded in his field. Leah was five when her parents divorced, and her father's second wife was also a successful career woman before she retired.

Working feeds a deep-rooted need she has to contribute, an unexplainable need she has had since she was young. To her, it was so "important to try to earn money and not just [have it] be given to [her]" that she lied about her age to get a job at the local café scooping ice cream. This wasn't a requirement of her parents—it was a responsibility she assigned to herself. She describes it as something "nice to do given how hard they worked." This way of thinking was fairly pervasive for Leah. She attended a private school and wouldn't join her friends when they cut classes, but not because she feared getting into trouble and being sent to detention. Rather it was because she calculated how much each class cost and didn't want to waste any of her father's money. When I ask her about the source of her self-imposed vigilance, she says, "Oh, I don't know . . . there was almost like a subconscious gratefulness. . . . I didn't want them to feel that they were wasting [money] on me." I understood her response more fully when she disclosed that she and her older brother (who has since passed away) were adopted as infants.

This need to contribute did not stop with her parents—it has extended into her marriage as well. Hence, the reason she works part-time. In scaling down her work hours and, thus, salary, she and her husband, Armand, have exchanged roles. Once she was the major breadwinner, now he is. But regardless of who is earning the most, they have agreed that money will not be a bargaining chip. For them, she says, "the contributions don't have to be equal to count. . . . There's an equality that exists between us if we both contribute." As a result, "the issue of control does not come up when dealing with money" in their household. Nor does the typical yours versus mine mentality—everything is considered "ours."

Setting aside her personal preferences and their approach to handling money matters, there are economic realities driving Leah's choice to limit the degree to which she opts out. "I think our house is one of the things we went about a little bit naively. . . . We owned an apartment in Manhattan that was not at all a stretch for us financially. Now we live in a town that has the highest property taxes in all of New Jersey, and between the taxes and the actual cost of the home . . . it's been a surprise for us, and we didn't really understand how everything would add up." In addition to their house, there's the $13,000 preschool tuition for their four-year-old. "We've been paying property taxes while our son has been in a private pre-K. There would have always been the preschool expenses, but the taxes . . . it's a nice amount of money that we've paid that didn't have to be. Maybe we could have waited until we needed to be here because by the time he enters public school, we'll have lived here four and a half years. The property taxes don't feel so unbelievable when you are not also paying for private school."

While it is true that Leah must work, what is also true is that the weight of their suburban expenses, though manageable, is proving to be stressful. At times, the stress has caused Leah to feel self-conscious about her choice to step away from her high-powered, glamorous job that took her all over the world. "I still get a little panicked by the fact that I made that choice," she says. The anxiety she occasionally feels is a common inner struggle I've heard from women who opt out, and it is a sentiment a few of the women in Ms. Belkin's article gave voice to as well.

The reaction to a woman's personal choice to opt out has escalated into a social debate that is pitting those who can against those who cannot. It considers those who don't as bolstering women's gains in the workplace and those who do as undermining the efforts of the feminists who came before them. Leah reinforces this sad truth when she tells of a friend of hers who is uncomfortable telling people that she stays home. According to Leah, "She feels so embarrassed about being a stay-at-home mother that she recently said, 'I almost wish I had a job that was twenty hours [a week] so at least I could say that I'm doing something.'"

Leah's self-consciousness about her choice to work only part-time and her friend's admission of embarrassment highlight that when it comes to the opt-out revolution, there are three conversations happening simultaneously. There's the highly personal inner dialogue that frequently asks, "Did I make the right choice?" There's the one you have with trusted friends, and then there's the conversation you have with society at large and vice versa. The last two tap into a common anxiety: what will others think?

Figuring out what is right for you and your family is fluid, changing as your needs, wants, and responsibilities dictate. It is challenging because rarely are any of your decisions arrived at via a black-and-white decision-making process. There are always tradeoffs that land your decisions squarely—even if not so neatly—in life's gray zone. I don't think couples come to the decision to have one of them (usually the wife) opt out without difficulty, even for families wherein the working spouse earns a sizeable income. There are career ramifications for the spouse stepping off a career track, especially if done during crucial career-building years. Likewise there are financial implications for the family when you scale down to one income from two.

Leah and Armand may not be able to hop a plane to go to Armand's hometown in Italy at the drop of a hat like they used to, or join friends for a week in Mexico without giving it a second thought as they have done in the past, but they also are not living in survival mode. The financial stress Leah feels is real for her, and it could easily be alleviated if she had more clients, worked more hours, or charged more for the work she does. However, exercising the first two options defeats the reason she chose to scale down in the first place. Besides, they are, to me, too one-dimensional to really address the issue at hand: her desire to be more present for her husband and toddler. "I want to be able to take [my son] to school and pick him up at the end of the day. . . . I want to be able to participate in his life. . . . For me, the whole love and money thing goes that way [as well]."

Christine

"We've been married for so long, and it's only in the last five or six years that we've really reached a balance of, I wouldn't say power, but a balance of family as to who's responsible for what," says Christine. She and Max met in 1990, were engaged six months later, and married in 1991. Theirs is a story of how life doesn't always unfold as you had envisioned and how sometimes you do really have to figure it out as you go along, all the while hoping that because you stuck with it, it will work out.

Christine grew up on the New Jersey Shore in a Victorian-style hotel-cum-house; the hotel rooms—with door numbers intact—served as the bedrooms for her, her thirteen siblings, and their parents. Her father's first wife, with whom he had eight children, died young and suddenly. He married Christine's mother when the children from his first marriage were all under the age of ten (can you imagine?), and they had six more children in succession, for a total of seven girls and seven boys. Christine is the twelfth child.

There is a lightness in Christine's voice as she describes the idyllic surroundings of her childhood—a house on the water and a view of the New York City skyline, a place that has been beckoning her since she was ten years old. I sense the lightness intensifying as I listen to her talk about the parents she adored and her brothers and sisters. All of them are very close, and despite living along the East Coast from Florida to Vermont, they make it a point to get together once a year.

She sounds like someone who appreciates the effort her parents put forth "to make it look easy" when she knows it could not have been. Her father started work at seventeen at AT&T, in the mailroom. He joined the Navy after the bombing of Pearl Harbor, and after World War II returned to AT&T where he worked until he retired forty-five years later. By then he was a mid-level manager working in the accounting department. Christine doesn't have any records, but she suspects that her father never made more than $50,000 per year. In other words, "He didn't make a lot of money in relationship to the number of mouths he had to feed."

Christine's mother served in the army in the Women's Army Corps. She was introduced to Christine's father by his brother, who was also in the army. Indicative of the times, plus the immediate family of eight children and eventually six more that she would give birth to, she was a stay-at-home mom. And from what I can gather, she was a sexy and spirited stay-at-home mother who told her daughters not with words but in her actions to be more than a wife and a mother.

Christine's mother was extremely active in the PTA, and when the kids got older, she started working at the local five-and-dime store. She moved on to the local pharmacy, where she met the mayor, who also worked there. She got involved in local politics, first as a council member and then as the town's tax collector. She served in that capacity for twenty years until she retired.

In her parents, both of whom died in 2005, Christine saw teamwork at its best. Both of them were very good with money; both had perfect credit scores; both were savers and brought their children up to be savers as well; and both were organized and meticulous. (After her parents' death, Christine and a sister found one of her mother's ledgers from Christmas 1963 with the boys on one side and the girls on the other. She was tracking how much each gift cost and how much was left on the layaway balance at the five-and-dime store.) Christine doesn't know which is more accurate, that they "made money appear when it was needed, or that they allowed us to have a life that wasn't centered around money so we didn't notice when it wasn't there." But what she does know is that her parents worked hard to create a full life for their children despite not having much money.

Her parents' marriage and the way in which they handled money have had a profound effect on Christine. "I was very fortunate to come of age with a very strong mother and a father who appreciated her strength and valued her contribution financially and emotionally to the family. You know, that was a great example for me in terms of finding a husband myself who *eventually* also felt the same way."

Just as Christine's uncle introduced her parents, her sister introduced her to Max, the man who would become her husband. Like Christine, Max moved to New York City to pursue his dreams. He, however, traveled a much longer distance—from Morocco. As is the case with most developing countries, there is a great disparity between the rich and the poor. Max's family is on the rich side. His father worked as a high official with the Moroccan government and "kept a pretty, pretty long shadow." Wanting to be on his own, Max moved first to Quebec, but he found it too cold. He sold his belongings and migrated to New York City "without a job and barely even any English." He, like Christine and every other young dream chaser, was naive enough to think it would all work out and refused to let details stop him.

Three years after his arrival in 1987, he met Christine. When they got together they were both working and "making a lot of cash," which afforded them the ability to take advantage of all that New York City had to offer. He was working in the restaurant industry as a bartender and waiter; she in the garment industry on the wholesale side. When they got together, she was making $70,000 per year and was bored out of her mind. With Max's full support, she made a career change and decided to try the retail side of the business.

But retail, especially in a commission-only environment, is much different than wholesale, and her income dropped significantly at just the wrong time. As is characteristic of life, there was a perfect storm of events: just as they were adjusting to her new, lower salary, there was a shift in Max's work, and he wasn't bartending as much. They went from earning a lot separately and together and living a very carefree lifestyle to struggling. Just then she found out she was pregnant with their first child.

She returned to the wholesale side of the business and began working for a high-end fashion designer. It was a full salary position that provided security, a steady paycheck, and much-needed health insurance. However, it didn't match the wholesale salary she previously earned—it paid just $35,000 a year. The struggle continued, now more than ever, because they were living off her salary, Max was at home with the baby, and there was another one on the way.

A confluence of events brought about another shift, this time in a more positive direction. She met Robbin, a woman who became her mentor, sponsor, and chief advocate. As Christine describes it, Robbin "plucked me from obscurity and managed my career and turned everything around for me." She saw that Christine was smart, talented, and fighting hard for her family. With Robbin guiding her career and fighting on her behalf, Christine's salary more than doubled within eighteen months. Christine shared these details to demonstrate the arc of not only her career but how she and Max "went from rolling quarters to buy milk to being able to make it through the month without sweating."

She and Robbin both continue to work for the same company, and Robbin coaches her from a distance, but Christine no longer reports directly to her. Today, Christine is running a multi-million-dollar division and earning a high-six-figure salary, joining the ranks of women who earn more than $100,000. (According to the Bureau of Labor Statistics, the number of women with earnings greater than $100,000 has quadrupled in the last decade.) Max is a stay-at-home dad, and although he has a business importing olive oil from Morocco and it is self-sustaining, none of its revenues are used to handle any of the household's finances. As such, Christine is one of the thirty-seven million women who in 2005 were the major breadwinners for their families.

Christine and Max are still dealing with lingering debt from when times were tough, but they are no longer struggling. Yet, she confesses, "I have to emotionally catch up with the power that my money can have." And although, money is less of a "third rail" in their marriage today than it was in years past, it can still be a precarious area on occasion. "You have every great intention of being able to face an issue without going back in time and saying, 'Oh, you did this and you should've done that,' or 'I did that and should've done this,' and regretting decisions that were made or not made in many cases. You want to be able to discuss [money] in a mature, detached, unemotional way, but you just can't."

They both had a feeling that "whether [they] could afford it or not, somebody had to stay home once [they] had kids," even though they never actually talked about it or tried to define how it would work out. Their boys are now eleven and nine, and Max has been home with them from the beginning. She jokes and says, "We didn't set out with a plan, and had we talked about it, it probably would have been to our own detriment." For them, they naturally found a groove, one that was predicated on "a lot of compromise and long stretches of time when neither was happy but too overwhelmed to even think about divorce."

Interestingly, their money challenges have never centered on the fact that she is the major breadwinner—that has not been an issue for either of them. From her perspective, she says, "I just thought it would always be a partnership. . . . In my mind, there's so much work to be done in a relationship and in a family that everybody has to do something, and you can't define it so narrowly." As for Max, she says, "He's just happy somebody's getting it done." When I ask her if Max is comfortable with the label "stay-at-home dad," she responds, "I don't know if he would be comfortable with the label—it's such an American thing anyway—but he's definitely comfortable with the role." For them, their challenge with money is due to something far more subtle.

The entire household is managed from her income. She pays all the standard household bills like rent, cable, and phone directly from her checking account. She also handles any non-standard expenses as well, like buying a birthday gift for one of the boys' parties, giving them spending money for their play-dates, and taking the family out for dinner or a movie. Each week, Christine gives Max $500 for typical weekly household expenses like grocery shopping, paying the cleaning lady, the laundry, and dry cleaners. But this "transaction" often turns into a bone of contention because she will sometimes forget to go to the bank. When that happens he feels like she's being controlling and manipulative. In her mind, she just forgot to go the bank because "I didn't even leave my desk all day to go to the bathroom and I was trying to rush home to see the kids and help with homework." It is always on her to-do list; she just doesn't get to it every time. To me, theirs is a classic case of the intention of one person bumping up against the perception of another.

If money were just about the mechanics, this could easily be solved. However, it would require they do something Christine doesn't want to do. When she and Max got married, they had a joint checking account. But about five years ago, when they went through a really rocky period and she thought they were going to divorce, she set up her own checking account. Even though he wants her to change this arrangement and go back to having a joint account, she hasn't done it.

Who knows if she'll ever reach the point where she is ready and willing to share an account with Max again. But she remains unwavering in her commitment to continue fighting for her family, providing for them in a consistent way without putting any burden on them, and making it look as easy for her sons as her parents did for her and her thirteen siblings.

One way she is doing that is by remaining grounded. As she says, "I have a great story for my high school reunion. I live in Manhattan. I have a prominent address [she lives on Madison Avenue]. I work for a prominent designer, and my husband is from a foreign country." She continues, "But as my mother would say, 'Don't get too big for your britches.' At the end of the day, I'm just an Irish girl from Jersey trying to make a buck."

Shari

We know there are different levels of wealth in America, which are very broadly categorized as upper, middle, and working classes. We also know that even within these groupings there are tranches further subdividing our social class structure. But just as we tend to not have substantial and significant conversations about money, we tend to speak even less about social class in America. The conversations we are inclined to have about socioeconomic differences, segmentation, and awareness gingerly, at best, and abrasively, at worst, pit the have-had-longer against the newly minted haves and the have-nots.

Given the stereotypical way in which we usually talk about money and social class, we often miss the opportunity to truly explore the human dynamics of social class and the profound ways in which social class and money impact personal, particularly romantic, relationships. Spotting the obvious differences, such as rich versus poor or college-educated versus high-school graduate is fairly simple. The more subtle and nuanced differences are harder to identify, especially when you cross social class by way of marriage.

I met Shari through a mutual friend. I was curious about her and wanted to interview her for the book because I knew she was a stay-at-home mother with two children, one of whom has special needs. I didn't know of her family's wealth when I met her, nor was I aware of it when I asked if I could interview her.

Shari and her family remind me of some of the private banking families with whom I worked first at Bankers Trust and then at my firm, Sterling Investment Management. Unlike some clients with whom I have worked, she doesn't flaunt her wealth; her self-description, "I'm pretty low-key," is definitely accurate. But in New York City, there are certain words that give you clues as to the degree of someone's wealth even if their carriage is modest. Words such as "Sutton Place," "Fifth Avenue," "Dalton," "East Hampton," "nanny," and "maid."

She met Jonathan, her husband of nine years, in law school. He didn't know of her family's wealth initially, either. He discovered it after they had been dating a while, when he met her father for the first time. They went to her dad's apartment on Fifth Avenue—where the elevator opens right into the apartment overlooking Central Park. "I know that I warned him on the way over, like, 'just so you know' kind of thing." It was the first time Jonathan had ever been to such an apartment. For Shari and her older sister, the wealth and financial comfort her father's apartment represents is all they have ever known.

Two years after her mother died, her father relocated the family from Westchester to Manhattan, a move that brought them closer to both sets of grandparents. One set lived on Sutton Place; the other also on Fifth Avenue. Shari entered the seventh grade at the Dalton School, a private school simply called "Dalton" by New Yorkers.

Shari's father is an attorney by trade, but a serial entrepreneur by profession. Being an entrepreneur was encouraged by his own father, who was a self-employed accountant and who didn't believe in working for someone else. For many years, her father had a private law practice, and then he ventured into several other business enterprises including commercial real estate development.

For as long as Shari can remember, her father has been successful and always at ease with letting his girls know that their family was comfortable. At the same time, "He was not showy or excessive." Shari and her sister grew up with a maid and nanny, which they probably would have had even if their father weren't a single dad. They also grew up with a father who was home every night for dinner. Even when they spent time at their summer house in East Hampton, "there was someone there cooking for us, but if you walked into the house we'd all be sitting around in jeans. . . . To this day that's kind of what the atmosphere is like."

Shari and her sister had the luxury of growing up wanting for nothing. Yet, she says, "Somehow my sister and I did not grow up as spoiled children. I think because our dad was very generous we didn't feel like we needed to ask for so many things." Their father's generosity gave Shari the opportunity "to spend every summer in high school working at a camp for autistic and emotionally disturbed kids and college summers working at a camp for underprivileged children." She continues by saying, "I always did a lot of community service, and I feel like those are the kinds of thing we were able to do because of our financial situation."

Her father's generosity and the family's financial situation have also put Shari in an enviable position: she has never had to work to support herself. She has not worked to earn money since giving birth five and a half years ago to her eldest son. After law school, she went to work for Legal Aid—something some of her friends would have liked to do as well but "didn't have the luxury of being able to do." It is certainly a luxury Jonathan never had.

Unlike Shari and her sister, who worked because they wanted to, doing work that was meaningful to them, "Jonathan worked at the supermarket during the summers of high school and college because he had to." After law school, he joined a big law firm, a path he likely would have stayed on were it not for the choices he is now able to explore because he is married to Shari.

In 2005, the *New York Times* ran an eleven-piece series exploring how class influences destiny in America. As part of the series, Tamar Lewin wrote an article exploring cross-class marriage, "When Richer Weds Poorer, Money Isn't the Only Difference." What made it unusual was that it profiled a couple wherein the wife was rich and the husband was poor. Normally, our culture, whether in literature or movies, pays more attention to cross-class marriages of rich, educated men marrying poor, less-educated women. What made the article usual is that the differences between the couple were really, really stark. She was from a family whose name adorns city buildings. Everyone in her family is Ivy League educated. And she works in philanthropy as a means of dealing with her feelings of guilt regarding her inherited wealth. Her husband, on the other hand, is from a working-class family where no one went to college and everyone's goal was to get a good job in the local factory, and he is a high school dropout who eventually joined the navy. Once discharged, he worked a variety of jobs. His job as a car salesman is how they met.

The article details the typical issues that arise in cross-class marriages, such as who has more options and power, and who makes the most decisions. Plus, it showcases the challenges the couple, Dan Croteau and Cate Woolner, have experienced integrating their respective families and the delicate line they each walk when dealing with each other's children from earlier marriages concerning money. Something I was surprised to learn about, but glad to know exists, are workshops on cross-class relationships. Before getting married, Dan and Cate attended a series that Dan calls "useful." Though initially reticent about attending, he says, "I think we would have made it anyway, but we would have had a rockier time without the [classes]."

Jonathan comes "from a solidly middle-class family." His dad is also a lawyer who specializes in estate planning and is successful in a different way than Shari's father is. Jonathan was lucky in that his parents paid for college and his grandparents paid for law school. But his family and Shari's are in different categories. There's wealth, and then there's ultra-wealth. Shari and Jonathan had a big, fancy, ultra-wealthy wedding at the Plaza Hotel. "For his family and friends, they had never been to an event like that," Shari says. For her family and friends, it was common.

Shari and Jonathan each have a juris doctorate, and both of their fathers are lawyers. When it comes to the standard ways cross-class relationships are measured—education, occupation, income, and wealth—they have much more in common than Dan and Cate from the *New York Times* article. The areas of stark difference for them, income and wealth, bring to mind the dynamics of "new money" versus "old money." Both instances require managing a potentially combustible combination of psychological baggage and preconceived notions, which makes me wonder: how do you handle the nuances that arise when what is "old" money to you is "new" money to your spouse?

"Marriages that cross class boundaries may not present as obvious a set of challenges as those that cross the lines of race or nationality," Lewin states in her article.[12] But the challenges they do pose are probably equally complicated from an emotional standpoint. In Shari and Jonathan's case, the complications are obscure.

In terms of their money management styles, Shari and Jonathan are in sync. They are both conservative spenders; she has to encourage him to spend money on himself or spend the extra money to purchase direct flight tickets as opposed to the cheaper ones that involve a change of planes. As for herself, she'll buy a sandwich but not a drink; "I feel so psyched that I didn't spend a $1 on a soda." Likewise, she could easily afford to spend $1,000 on the latest handbag, but she considers that excessive. "I feel happy that I can do things that I enjoy, that I can afford to do things that really give me pleasure, and that certain challenges in my life are much easier because I have finances that I can count on." But spend $1,000 on a handbag? "I would never do that." That said, she reveals, "We're [also] similar in that we are not strict in terms of how much money we're spending exactly. . . . We're probably not as aware of it as we could be but, [Jonathan] is much more knowledgeable about what we do with our money and how we invest it. He's much more interested in it and involved with it and thus communicates more with our private banker." Similarly, they are both extremely grateful for her resources because "having money has really been helpful in terms of meeting the needs of our eldest son, who has special needs." She continues, "Money definitely cannot buy happiness, but it can make your life easier. . . . There are a lot of things that we couldn't have done or that would have made it even harder . . . so lucky for us that we can make a tough situation a little bit easier."

According to Shari, she and her sister "genuinely married men who are not really so impressed by [their] wealth. . . . They are not caught up in it." Still, the same money that is a blessing for them can sometimes be tricky for them as well. They live in a very comfortable, beautiful apartment that is nicer than Jonathan's salary could afford. But as he told her, "I'm not going to ask you to live in a small, cramped place that I could afford just for my ego." Additionally, Shari's family wealth has given him a flexibility he could never have envisioned as possible before their marriage. "He has struggled to find a job that is both meaningful and lucrative; he wants to feel good and proud of what he's doing." He has yet to find the right fit.

Shari is supportive of him exploring his options until he does, though she admits, "It would be exciting in a different way to spend money that he made—more for him because I think it weighs on him. I think he likes the fact that he doesn't have to work somewhere where he's not happy simply to make money. But I think there are times when he wishes that he was bringing in the money that was allowing us to do certain things. And sometimes I feel that might be a good thing for us because it might somehow balance things in certain ways."

Bells and Whistles Without the "Paper"

Mary Anne

Mary Anne is in her late thirties, has never been married, and doesn't have any children. She has a fulfilling career, and until recently, she enjoyed the nomadic lifestyle it demanded. Two years ago, she met Sebastian, a man she wants to settle down with and settle down for. While she has had other relationships, they were never as serious to her as the one she has with Sebastian. It is this relationship that has ignited desires in her she had not had heretofore; it is this relationship that has her trading in long stints on the road and time spent in various airports and hotels, on airlines, and living out of suitcases, for a place she calls home. One that includes someone on the other side of the door.

Wanting to nest and stop spending so much time on the road is just one of a handful of firsts for Mary Anne when it comes to her relationship with Sebastian. For the first time, she is living with someone, even going so far as moving across the country to be with him. For the first time, she's letting someone in on the not-so-pretty details of her financial life—though this wasn't necessarily by choice. The source of all of these firsts: "This is something I really, really want," she says.

Being in a committed, romantic relationship is all about getting close and letting someone in. When that happens, the other person eventually sees your "stuff"—that which you intentionally disclose as well as what they are able to piece together from what they observe. Hiding becomes almost impossible in an intimate relationship, especially when your living space is shared.

Mary Anne provides consulting services to the healthcare industry, and the first quarter of every year is slow; it's an industry phenomenon and something she has grown accustomed to after nineteen years. She doesn't own any investments and doesn't have much in the way of savings. "You'd think I would save more, but I keep thinking, 'Nope, [the slow period] isn't going to happen.'" Yet it does, and each time whatever she has managed to save is used to pay her bills and pull her through the first three months of each year.

At the top of this year, what usually worked in the past backfired.

Sebastian and Mary Anne dated for eight months, broke up for as many months, and got back together. Prior to them reuniting, she had plastic surgery on her nose and breasts. She paid for these procedures with her American Express card. Shortly afterward, she got a notification from the Internal Revenue Service that she owed taxes. The company she worked for prior to starting her own business had not been taking out taxes for all of the states in which she worked throughout the year—for three years! She used her American Express card to pay this tax obligation, too. At the same time, she decided to go into practice for herself and contract directly with clients as opposed to working for the consulting company. She put her business start-up costs on her American Express card. In a matter of three months, she had added $44,000 to the balance she already had.

She had had debt before and worked her way out of it. She figured she'd be able to do the same in this instance. But soon she found herself traveling down an unfamiliar path. In addition to the new year getting off to a slow start, she didn't earn as much in the fourth quarter as she had in previous years. Her American Express account went into collections, and they threatened to freeze her bank account since she didn't have employee wages to garnish. She got the call from American Express stating such as she was driving across the country to California.

"I didn't want [anyone] to know about my bills and have to share information and how I choose to live," is one of the reasons Mary Anne cites as to why she never chose to live with anyone before. She hadn't even arrived, and yet the first thing she'd have to do before she got a chance to settle into her new life living with Sebastian is tell him (another first) about the Amex situation, since she knew it was going to prevent her from being able to pay the amount they had agreed would be her portion of the household bills. He didn't mind, but he was perplexed. A few months after her arrival, he saw her struggling, which he hadn't seen when she was living on the East Coast renting a condo valued at $2.5 million.

Almost from the time she arrived in Southern California, Sebastian would say, "Mary Anne, you have to tell me how much debt you have left on your credit card. I want us to buy a house at the end of the year or next year." At first, she skirted the question. But sensing she couldn't defer an answer any longer, she finally told him three months after her arrival. He asked, "How the *hell* did you get to that point when last year you were doing really well?" She gave him the details about the plastic surgery, taxes, and start-up costs, and he continued by asking, "You earned $40,000 from one client. Why weren't you able to wipe out those debts immediately? Where did the money go?" *She didn't know.* And when he asked to see her accounts receivable, she couldn't produce a report because she didn't keep track of her accounts receivable on paper. It was in her head.

Sebastian was very upset, and he was not bashful about expressing it. He told her more than once, "I'm so disappointed in you." Of all the things she is experiencing for the first time in her relationship with him, his reaction to her money woes was not one she had anticipated or particularly liked. Not because she thought his reaction was wrong (though she would have preferred a different tenor), but because to him, she "didn't care what went on." And he wasn't entirely off base with his assessment. Mary Anne readily admits that she never really thought about money. For her, "it was never a big issue," that is, until her relationship with Sebastian, the first that has ever prompted her to think seriously and strategically about her financial future. "He is so money-conscious," she says, that being with him has made her very aware of what she does and doesn't do with money. It has inspired her to want to do the "right" things.

On this front, she's not off to the greatest of starts: he thinks her total debt obligation is $44,000; it's actually *$70,000*. Based on his response to what she did tell him, she's glad she didn't reveal the *whole* truth and now regrets that she even shared what she did—especially in light of the friction her disclosure has caused. According to Mary Anne "it's changed things intimately."

Couples choose to live together for myriad reasons. Sometimes it's for convenience; sometimes it's to conserve money; sometimes it's to test the waters before marriage. Regardless of the reason behind the choice, living together has evolved into a family structure that is just as viable as a traditional marriage, especially now that it no longer carries the social stigma it once did. By 2000, the total number of unmarried couples in America was almost 4.75 million, up from less than half a million in 1960. The increasing numbers seem to go hand in hand with the increased "social and legal identification (of cohabitation) as a distinct new institution."[13] But, as Mary Anne is discovering, people who live together must navigate the same financial waters as married couples whose financial choices affect one another. (And if couples who live together do not sign a domestic partnership agreement, they join their lives and their finances without any of the built-in protections of a marriage license.)

Mary Anne and Sebastian's foray into living together didn't have the fairy-tale beginning she had envisioned, but it has been a tremendous learning opportunity—about him, about him and her, and about the degree to which she is truly a modern, independent woman. Despite the trappings of a college education, a lucrative career and business, and access to information to help her manage her money and business well, she says, "Maybe I don't know what an independent woman is." She goes on to say, "I don't think people know what an independent woman is. When I think about the ability to pay or the choice to pay —which is how I've come to redefine and measure my independence—I realize I don't have either right now." To make matters worse, she says, "I never thought I'd be living my mother's same lifestyle. I'm making a heck of a lot more than she has ever earned, and yet I am still struggling."

With our country in the midst of one of its most significant credit crises to date and the American consumer debt load at an all-time high, there isn't a dearth of news reports about the financial challenges a vast majority of people are facing. However, rarely do those stories uncover the backstory to shed light on the emotional cost of debt. Debt you cannot manage affects your self-esteem and sense of validation, and if you are seeking approval from a mate who frowns upon nonessential debt, in general, and how you manage money, in particular, it affects the degree to which you feel accepted by that person.

Mary Anne has full confidence in her ability to pay off her $70,000 debt. She wishes Sebastian had as much faith in her. "I honestly believe if he did, he wouldn't be as disappointed as he is, and I wouldn't see [this situation] as such a failure because I think that's how he sees it." Knowing then that this is how she feels, it totally breaks my heart to hear her say, "I'm not comfortable around him [anymore]. . . . I think our friends envy the couple we present to the outside world, but I don't think they'd envy us behind closed doors."

That is the true cost of debt: its insalubrious impact on relationships.

Sasha

When Oscar Wilde said, "The truth is rarely pure and never simple," he undoubtedly tapped into a profound understanding of the complicated and often complex nature of human relationships. I wonder what sparked this awareness. Was he or someone close to him rationalizing a choice that had had unintended consequences? Did it seep into his consciousness as he reflected on a lie told to him, or one he told someone? One thing is for sure: Mr. Wilde's insightful statement is an apt way to describe the financial paradoxes of Sasha's life.

Imagine one of your memories from childhood is that your family frequently ran out of common consumer care products such as shampoo, toothpaste, bandages, and over-the-counter medicines, yet your father was a highly paid marketing executive at a pharma company where executives had free access to all the products the company created. Or that bill collectors frequently called your house, yet your parents drove a Bentley. The extremes make these contradictions seem absurd until you embrace the fact that we all grew up with (and live with still today) unexplainable incongruities.

Imagine you and your husband have two apartments, one of which is in South Beach. You discover that he has sold that condo when you show up for your condo association's standing board meeting and surprised board members greet you with, "Why are you here?"

Things are not always what they seem. And to me, your greatest financial risk is not the textbook definition of the term but the *illusion* that you have or know something you do not.

Sasha's now ex-husband's decision revealed that the transparency and trust she thought existed weren't really there. And either Sasha's parents didn't pay attention to details or the family's wealth wasn't as much as she presumed given other aspects of her experience growing up. Financial paradoxes are not new to Sasha. But nothing in her history, including what she witnessed growing up or experienced with her ex-husband, Miguel, could prepare her for the situation in which she finds herself with her live-in boyfriend, Jamal. "I never, ever, ever thought I would be in a situation where I'm sitting up here taking care of him, my two kids, and sometimes his two. I would say to myself, 'Something's really wrong with me.'"

The wealth in Sasha's family may not have been what she (or outsiders) thought, but they did have means. She may have occasionally gone without necessities like toothpaste and toilet paper, but very little else. Her parents didn't skimp when it came to exposing her and her sister to different cultures or when it came to financing their education. They both attended prestigious colleges and law schools. And unlike most students who arrive at college with luggage from the local department store, Sasha's mother insisted she have a Louis Vuitton luggage set. (She still has the set, some twenty-plus years later!)

Almost immediately after law school, Sasha got married to a man of means. For the first several years of their marriage, she was a housewife. She didn't work, yet she had the freedom to spend whatever amount of money she wanted on whatever she wanted. Having inherited what she calls her parents' tendency to "spend out of emotion" as well as their taste for luxury, she bought a lot of designer clothes, went to all the trendy restaurants, and traveled extensively. Miguel never once constrained her spending.

Sasha didn't have to work, but she wanted them to buy another house, and she wanted to contribute to the down payment. So, at the age of thirty she went to work for the first time since graduating law school. It was the first time she paid taxes. Imagine that! While she was in school, her father claimed her on his taxes; when she got married, her husband claimed her on his. Sure, she signed the tax forms every April, but she, herself, had not paid taxes until that point.

Before they reached their goal of buying a new house, though, Sasha became pregnant with their first daughter. It cut short her time as an employee. She gave birth to their second child, another girl, a year and half after their first child was born. When the youngest was three years old, Sasha decided it was time to kick-start her law career, and she's been working ever since.

Looking back, Sasha says, "The beginning of our problems was when he sold the apartment without telling me; financially he just wouldn't share with me because he didn't feel he had to." She didn't even know his salary when they got married. He was faithful to their marriage in all ways except when it came to money. His financial infidelity became emblematic of disconnects in other areas of their marriage. After twelve years, she and Miguel divorced.

Imagine, after being taken care of first by your father and then by your husband, finding yourself in a complete role reversal taking care of your live-in boyfriend. You didn't plan to have him move in with you and your children, and you certainly didn't intend to financially support him. Yet, this is the position Sasha now finds herself in with Jamal.

When they started dating four years ago, her divorce was final, but he was in the midst of a very ugly, protracted one of his own. She was working at a job she loved, earning a very good salary, and receiving child support. This combination enabled her to hold on to the other house she and Miguel eventually bought, and to maintain the lifestyle to which she and her daughters had become accustomed.

But then she lost her job. Though she got a three-year payout, she didn't adjust her living expenses or request an upward modification in child support. Around the same time, Jamal's divorce proceedings seriously deteriorated. His soon-to-be ex-wife had all his assets and income attached, including income and bonuses he had earned but was scheduled to receive at a later date. He had no earnings, no place to live, and no means of taking care of his children on the weekends he had them.

Sasha's response was to help him out. "What am I supposed to do? I have money. How could I not do whatever I could to help him out?" She continues, "Suppose this were my situation, and it was the other way around, and I was the one who needed help? I wouldn't want someone to leave me stranded."

She didn't leave Jamal stranded when she had money, and she hasn't done so during this period when she doesn't have much of it, either. The funds from her three-year payout didn't last as long as she had planned—and instead of looking for a job during this time, she started a business that is just now beginning to generate revenue. But it was too late to prevent her from having to sell the house she loved earlier this year in a short-sale transaction to avoid foreclosure.

It shows up differently for each of us, but to some extent, we all come to our romantic relationships a bit handicapped when it comes to navigating the money and love terrain. For Sasha, it showed up in terms of financial wisdom and maturity; she didn't have enough of either to sufficiently engage either Miguel or Jamal in constructive conversations about money before, during, or after it surfaced as a problem they would have to work through. She and Jamal have recently begun to have those "awkward" conversations, right when patience and understanding are about as empty as both of their bank accounts.

I ask her if she would make the same choice to support Jamal if she could do it over again. Sasha provides a qualified yes, a yes with some predetermined boundaries. Supporting Jamal and sometimes his two children has put an extra drain on her financial resources and thus a drain on their relationship. "Love with no money is no fun," she says. She feels so strongly about this that she's decided to tell her daughters to "make sure that the mate you choose has similar financial goals and that you discuss financial goals before you get married." In other words, don't go into romantic and financial relationships blindly. And obviously, I couldn't agree more.

Although I completely understand the rationale for opting out of marriage, especially if you or your mate has been previously married, I typically advocate for marriage over cohabitation. My reasons are not entirely morally based; the financial risks when you are unmarried are greater. Whether you are married or living with someone, your financial challenges inevitably become entwined. Your partner's financial challenges become yours and vice versa. But unlike with marriage, where you have some level of financial protection and recourse if necessary, living with someone leaves you completely vulnerable unless you have a domestic partnership agreement, which most unmarried, heterosexual couples do not.

I firmly believe that the seed for all paradoxes, financial or otherwise, are untruths or half-truths. It could be the case that someone wasn't honest with you, you weren't honest with him or her, or you weren't honest with yourself. At times, the lack of honesty is unintentional and most likely the result of pre-tense; other times, it is deliberate and most likely the result of a premeditated omission. We tend to pay more attention to the latter and less to the former. But either way, we frequently only recognize them for what they are *after* the fact and usually after the damage has been done.

Girl Meets Girl

Miriam and Robin

At the height of both the civil rights and women's movements, there were some people who still thought blacks and women should stay in their "places." Desegregation laws were enacted to encourage people to do what they perhaps would not do on their own effort, naturally. The truth is no social movement has ever been fully embraced nor the change it endeavored to foster welcomed by all with open arms. That includes the current gay rights movement. In writing this section, I don't presume everyone reading it is in support of the gay and lesbian population or same-sex couples. And, in writing this profile, I don't presume everyone is accepting of the latest issue to stir up a great deal of debate: children of same-sex couples.

I do take a particular liberty in presuming, however, that every reader would agree that children shouldn't get caught in the middle of ideological differences between adults. Case in point: Marcus was innocently asked by a fellow student about his mother and father; he responded just as innocently, "I have two mothers." "A 7-year-old Louisiana boy [was] disciplined by his elementary school for telling a second-grade classmate [during recess] that he had two mothers and explaining that gay meant 'when a girl likes a girl,' says the American Civil Liberties Union (ACLU),"[14] was the opening paragraph of an article that ran in the *New York Times* on December 3, 2003. According to the article, the teacher scolded Marcus in front of his class, telling him *gay* was a bad word, and sent him to the principal's office. A copy of the Louisiana Department of Education School Behavior Report, which the ACLU was working to have removed from Marcus's school records, reveals that the teacher wrote, "I feel that parents should explain things of this nature to their own children in their own way."

Whereas others look at his family as *alternative*, all the little boy saw was his family. Two mothers were just as normal to him as a father and mother are to another child.

Using data from the U.S. Census Bureau, the Williams Institute compiled the following statistics: In 2000, there were 594,391 same-sex couples living in the U.S.[15] By 2005, the number of same-sex couples increased by more than 20 percent to 776,943.[16] There are more male same-sex couples than female-same sex couples, and 20 percent of same-sex couples in the U.S. are raising children under the age of eighteen.[17] These numbers seem abstract until you take into account that they are talking about Marcus and the thousands of other children like him with either two mommies or two daddies.

Abigail is another one of those children. She has two mommies, Miriam and Robin. She and her parents are three more faces behind the aforementioned statistics. She didn't do anything that would necessitate the involvement of the ACLU to protect her rights and freedoms, but what she did for her mothers was just as essential. "She really got us together, because we realized that we couldn't pussyfoot around anymore because we have a child to take care of," said Miriam. What is interesting about this statement is when it was said. It wasn't *after* the baby was born, which is when most people make comments about how much a baby has changed their lives. For Miriam and Robin, their moment of epiphany and the inspiration to change their financial ways came *before* their baby girl was even born!

Miriam and Robin started dating in 1998 and moved in together in 1999. They didn't learn the intricacies of each other's finances until 2001, the year in which both of their salaries were garnished for loans they had each taken out and run into difficulty repaying. Until this stressful moment, which was devastating financially as well as emotionally, they had never *really* talked about money.

Robin, who is black, grew up in the South Bronx. She didn't grow up rich, but she certainly felt financially safe and secure.

As she puts it, "I always felt taken care of." She goes on to add, "I never had hand-me-down clothes, and food was always on the table." She never felt she couldn't have anything, except designer stuff. (We both had a hearty laugh when I said, "Ah, your mother wouldn't let you have a pair of Jordache jeans?" The answer: no.)

Robin's issues with money began during her junior year in college, when she got her first credit card. She fell into the same trap as many of us who got credit cards during our college years without fully understanding the responsibility. Robin charged everything and anything because, as she saw it, "I'm going to make lots of money [when I graduate]." But she didn't have a reference point of what "lots" of money would be, since she had never worked, not even during the summers of high school or college.

Her carefree charging led to more debt than she could handle. But she was able to clear it up within a year with the help of a budget/credit counseling service. But then she did it again! "The second time around wasn't so great," she says, because it wasn't as easy to get back to zero. When she got into credit card trouble the first time, she was living at home—she didn't have any financial obligations other than paying her credit card bills. The second time was a different story. In addition to paying her credit card bills, she had rent and other bills to pay. It wasn't long before she began getting threatening calls from collection agencies, which horrified and scared her and left her near tears, asking "How do I get out of this?"

I, on the other hand, wondered how she got *into* her financial quandary, not just once but twice! Granted, money was never discussed, so she was never instructed about what to do or to avoid, but based on how she *saw* money being handled at home with her mother, grandmother, and, for a short while, her stepfather, it was clear she wasn't following the model set by them. She was forging a new path, just in the wrong direction.

When Robin's debt crisis was at its worst (so she thought), she met Miriam. Unbeknownst to her, Miriam was also in a heap of debt.

Miriam, who is white, grew up in Ohio with her mother and older brother. Her parents divorced when she was a little over two years old. All of her memories about money growing up can be aptly summed up in one word: horrible. She remembers going to the refrigerator and finding that everything was warm because the electricity was turned off. She remembers the frequent calls to the house from bill collectors. She remembers never having any money and never, ever having anything new; her toys and clothes were all used. "I remember wanting to have things I couldn't have," she says.

Miriam and her mother were poor in part because her father didn't pay child support; he and her mother were in a custody battle that lasted eighteen years. Additionally, her mother was a doctoral student and didn't have a job with income until Miriam was eight years old. At that time, her mother started working as a professor in Brooklyn, which alleviated some but not all of the financial pressure. As Miriam puts it, "My mom was terrible with money." So at a young age, Miriam became the "adult" and took care of paying the bills and making sure they were paid on time.

All of this is intriguing when you consider the life of Miriam's maternal grandmother. She immigrated to America from Russia in 1920 with nothing. She was the youngest of a family of eleven and didn't speak any English. Her husband, Miriam's grandfather, worked as a manager in a bra factory on the Lower East Side of Manhattan, and from his check she saved and invested all the money she could. She and her husband lived very frugally, and they amassed quite a fortune. When Miriam's mother was a student, her grandmother often sent money to help out. And when she died she *really* helped out. After her death, they learned that the grandparents had multiple bank accounts, investments, and several properties. A sizeable inheritance was bequeathed to Miriam's mother.

Today, Miriam's mother is very wealthy because of what was willed to her, not because her mother passed down her insight and know-how in terms of investing in stocks and purchasing investment property. Miriam doesn't want to wait until her mother dies before she begins to create her own wealth. As Miriam sees it, "My mom got all of this independence and happiness and ability to do things that she couldn't do for us on her own because of her inheritance." She adds, "I think that I've been trying all my adult life to be independent and to be able to deal with money and not have my mom's issues with money. And I've had some failures. I've had some debt issues. I've had some problems."

Miriam and Robin jokingly say, "We got together in debt." They have earned the right to joke, as they have come a long way in the last three years by making some hard choices.

Robin works as a therapist at a nonprofit organization and in private practice. Miriam is back to working as a teacher and is in the process of completing her doctoral studies. She worked as a teacher when she and Robin met, and supplemented her income during the summers and evenings by working as a real estate agent. The commission she earned was enough to replace her teacher's salary—since she was burnt out, she made a decision not to return to teaching in 2001. Then everything in New York City changed on September 11. People weren't buying real estate, so Miriam's income changed as well. "All of a sudden, my income went down." She didn't earn any income for the rest of the year. The timing could not have been worse; not only was she falling behind in making payments to her credit card lenders and for an outstanding personal loan, but so was Robin. What Robin was making at the time wasn't enough to cover all of her expenses. They were able to negotiate revised payment terms with all of their respective creditors, except with the credit union for the personal loan they each had. The credit union garnished their salaries.

This is when they moved into the apartment that would be critical to their plan to stop "pussyfooting" around. They rented an apartment from a landlord who didn't check their credit. The rent was $1,600. A year later, the landlord wanted to sell the apartment, and they negotiated a purchase price of $170,000. Miriam's mother helped them with the down payment. The purchase did what they wanted—it brought down the monthly expense. The mortgage and maintenance came in at $1,250.

Even with a savings of close to $400 a month, though, it wasn't enough because of the amount of debt they each had. The hard truth was that "we really couldn't afford to live there." They came to this realization when Robin got pregnant and they began to factor in how their expenses would increase even further once the baby was born.

Enter the master plan, devised by Miriam and bought into fully by Robin: sell the apartment they had grown to love so much! It was an extremely hard choice for them to make, but once they made it, everything afterward fell into place. Miriam did the necessary renovations to help increase the apartment's appeal, and they sold it themselves to save on the broker's fee. The apartment sold for $390,000, netting them $220,000 in profit, which "was used very carefully." They paid off all their debt, and what was left over was actually managed by their lawyers so that they would not have direct access to the funds. They even went so far as to have the lawyers send their monthly rent check directly to the new landlord. This arrangement, plus a strict budget, allowed them to both stay home and care for their daughter the first two years of her life.

Both of them say they "really learned a lot from staying home for two years." They became avid viewers of *The Suze Orman Show* on CNBC and learned a lot about money management. Robin goes on to add, "We went from two people coming together with debt, floundering around, and dealing with the stress debt causes in a relationship. But I feel like, even though it was difficult, we have learned along the way to be better with money and also to be able to talk about it."

Kim and Molly

Typically when two people get married, it is significant merely to the couple, their families, and their friends. Only when it comes to gay marriage do total strangers make their concerns known about whom a person is marrying.

Gay marriage is turning out to be one of the defining social change issues of the twenty-first century, challenging how we do and do not define marriage and family. You are almost guaranteed to ignite a spirited debate if you bring up gay marriage rights as a topic of discussion, even among gays and lesbians. The sentiments expressed, whether in support of or against, range from the political, social, and cultural, to the moral, philosophical, and religious. Future historians studying American legal, social, and political developments at the turn of the millennium will likely identify the debate over the legalization of same-sex marriage or same-sex civil unions as one of the defining domestic policy issues of the era.[18]

Americans have taken several giant steps for humankind recently, and they all speak to a tectonic shift that is underway. In April 2009, Iowa became the first state in the Midwest to legalize same-sex marriage and the fourth state overall, joining Massachusetts, Connecticut, and Vermont to deem the ban against same-sex marriage unconstitutional. In May 2008, the California Supreme Court struck down the ban on same-sex marriage, ruling the ban unconstitutional. Then, during the general election six months later, the ruling was reversed with the passage of Proposition 8; California's state constitution now only recognizes marriage between couples of opposite sexes, and select marriages between same-sex couples formed between June 2008 and May 2009.

Massachusetts, the first state to legalize same-sex marriages, made history again when it repealed a 1913 statute enacted in part to prevent interracial couples from evading their own state's ban by traveling to Massachusetts to marry. It was a little-used and rarely enforced law until opponents used it to prevent out-of-state gay couples from getting married in Massachusetts after the state legalized same-sex marriage in 2004.[19] On July 31, 2008, Deval Patrick, the governor of the state, signed into law a bill repealing the 1913 law, thereby permitting same-sex couples from other states to marry in Massachusetts, even if their marriages will not be recognized in their home states.

The 1996 Defense of Marriage Act (DOMA), signed by President Bill Clinton, denies federal recognition to same-sex marriages. As such, gay couples are precluded, on a federal level, from the 1,138 rights and obligations given to married heterosexual couples. Will the United States ever follow the lead of Denmark, the first country to legally sanction gay marriage almost twenty years ago? Only time will tell. But we know from history that federal and state laws can take a while to catch up with the evolution of their citizens. What makes California and Massachusetts as well as Vermont, Connecticut, New Jersey, New Hampshire, New York, and now Iowa stand out in terms of gay marriage rights is the stance these states have taken, and not without controversy, in light of DOMA. The laws in these states aren't just changing the legal landscape; they are changing the social landscape as well, reflecting the ever-evolving nature of our country.

And a changing social landscape is precisely why Kim and Molly can do something that was unfathomable thirty to forty years ago. Kim and Molly are joining the increasing number of lesbians proclaiming their love for and commitment to one another in the same way heterosexuals do: they are getting married!

What sets my interview of them apart from the others is that it is one of two where I interviewed both parties to the relationship. And during the course of our time together they provided confirmation of something I suspected but didn't know for certain: some of the financial concerns of same-sex couples are unique to them, but ultimately they encounter similar money and love challenges as male-female couples. For example, Kim and Molly, like some heterosexual couples, are also managing the dynamic of one person being the higher earner (Molly), and one being less engaged in the management of the household's finances (Kim). And they don't always see eye to eye.

Soon into our interview, I realized that I'd stumbled onto a rare relationship. In fact, several times I caught myself silently saying, "This can't be truly possible. How is it that they are as in sync as they seem to be and accepting of their differences to boot?" It isn't that some of the other people I interviewed don't have honesty, transparency, and directness in their relationships when it comes to money; it just seems that other couples work so hard to achieve and experience what Kim and Molly do with little effort.

All money, regardless of the currency and whether it is paper or coin, has two sides. I think this reminds us of the two aspects of money that are always present: the accounting side (the mechanics) and the psychology side (the emotions). Though Kim and Molly have to put forth "little effort," they are not precluded from putting forth *any* effort. And for them, their work shows up on the emotional side, especially when it comes to the issue of yours, mine, and ours.

Kim and Molly have a lot in common, which might explain the synchronicity on the accounting side. Here, in no specific order, are some of their similarities: have divorced parents; have fathers who are small business owners; grew up in middle-class, suburban neighborhoods; are Jewish; work for nonprofit organizations (Kim on the administrative side, Molly on the financial side); believe in living beneath their means; are self-described "common-sense spenders" and are debt-free; and are willing to talk through money issues when they surface.

One of Kim's earliest memories is hearing her parents fight about money. Perhaps because she was just six, they didn't think she knew what was going on, but she did. And when her parents divorced, money became even more of an issue. As a result, she can't ever recall not having to be mindful of money. This was further exacerbated when her mother remarried and relocated Kim and her younger sister to Quebec, Canada. Kim doesn't speak French, and getting a part-time job, even babysitting, proved to be a challenge. She wasn't able to start earning her own money until she graduated from college and returned to the United States. It was self-imposed, but she felt guilty asking either of her parents, especially her mother, for money. The guilt about spending money she doesn't view as her own continues to this day.

Molly's experience of her parents divorce couldn't be more opposite. While it was disruptive emotionally, it wasn't financially. She was aware of money growing up, but her consciousness of it doesn't come from a sense of struggle. It is because she comes from a family of means that highly values a strong work ethic. As such, Molly babysat a lot as a pre-teen, and as a teenager she started working in the family's business. Even though she knew she'd gain direct access to her trust fund when she turned thirty years old, that never stopped her from earning her own money, saving it, and making sure she made financially responsible and disciplined decisions.

Kim and Molly have been a couple for almost seven years and have lived together for four. By many standards, this is a long time. But there are some things that require more time to work out, even in the most communicative relationships.

They have a joint credit card, and they split shared expenses fifty-fifty. They split the household bills as well, but Molly pays a little bit more. She has always been the primary earner in their relationship, and she says, "I want [Kim] to feel like she has money for other things."

"Molly always says, 'What's mine is yours.' She means that one hundred percent, genuinely. But I have a big problem with that." And Kim adds, more as a stream of consciousness, "It's the way I was brought up. . . . I feel like I should provide for myself. . . . I feel like I still have this thing. You know, your money is your money, and my money is my money." Kim reminds us that knowing our baggage is one thing; being able to shake the residual effect of it is quite another. Such is the case with our experiences with money during our formative years.

Some examples that Kim and Molly shared in terms of when money highlighted an issue they had to talk through are traveling, joint banking accounts, and their respective feelings about the money they have jointly amassed.

They travel on at least one big vacation a year; last year's trip to Israel and Greece was the most expensive one to date. When Molly proposed the trip, Kim's initial response was, "Oh, that's a lot of money." Molly's solution was to pay for Kim's airfare, because to Molly, "it's more important to have [the] experience." It's the same for their upcoming wedding, which they've been saving for for three years. Molly is contributing more to that as well. She doesn't resent contributing more one bit; she's more than happy to do it. In her mind, whatever the additional monies are, "it's not a lot when you talk about how much money we make in a year and how many years we're going to work. It's fine." Kim is not totally comfortable yet with Molly paying more, but she is better than she was.

She is also still warming to the idea of having access to Molly's money when they open a joint banking account after the wedding. The thought of spending someone else's money is an idea she has to grow into.

Even if you take Molly's trust fund out of the equation, she and Kim are doing very well financially. Kim feels bad about the money they have and the money their friends don't have. Molly doesn't feel bad at all! She's grateful for her inheritance, saying, "I know how lucky I am, and I'm not squandering it. But I also know that I am very financially responsible. I have other money that I have saved all on my own."

Kim and Molly are giving themselves one of the best presents soon-to-be newlyweds can get: they are paying *cash* for their wedding. This is a gift that will have positive implications for many, many years to come. But by building a track record over the last seven years of being able to talk through absolutely anything and everything, they have already given to themselves one of the best gifts ever!

Liz

When I think about the world in which lesbians live today, I am reminded of the Virginia Slims ad campaign from 1978: "You've Come a Long Way, Baby." The slogan was designed to sell cigarettes, but it quickly caught on as a motto to underscore the progress women were making. The ad campaign was unveiled when I was thirteen, but what brought it to mind recently was a conversation with two women I met at an afternoon tea party.

It is almost impossible to get an accurate count, historically or currently, of the single gay and lesbian population in
the United States. The Census Bureau does not ask about sexual
orientation or count single gay, lesbian, and bisexual people. In
addition, the Census Bureau didn't start to collect data on same-
sex, unmarried partners until the 1990 census. These limitations
notwithstanding, it is estimated that there are nine million gay,
lesbian, and bisexual people (single and coupled) living in the
United States.[20]

Due to incomplete data, there really isn't a way to tell if
there are actually more lesbians today than in the past, but the
openness with which they live in the United States is certainly
greater today. The openness is mostly evident in two arenas. In
media and entertainment, there are a number of high-profile,
out celebrities, like Ellen DeGeneres, Melissa Etheridge, and
Rosie O'Donnell. And in corporate America, we are all aware of
workforce diversity initiatives. Ironically, corporate America is
on the forefront of many of the social changes concerning gay
rights. According to Joe Solmonese, president of the Human
Rights Campaign, "Corporate America is far ahead of America
generally when it comes to the question of equality for gay, lesbian, bisexual, and transgender (GLBT) people."[21]

But there is another reason why I know that lesbians are living more openly today than in the past, and it is far more personal. My mother is a lesbian. Part of the reason for wanting to
include a section about lesbians and female same-sex couples is
because I am fascinated with the openness with which lesbians
live and work today as compared to when my mother was the
age of the two openly gay women I met at the tea party. When
I listened to these women talking very candidly about the challenges they faced dating, free of any concerns of professional
ramifications or social stigmas, it occurred to me that this sense
of freedom is something that was never available to many of
the lesbians of the 1960s and '70s. My mother is far too private
a person to wear her sexual orientation on her sleeve; but putting aside her personal style about sharing such information,

she also came into the awareness of her sexuality at a time when one risked much to talk about it publicly. That may explain why she remained married to my father, at least on paper, until I was a teenager. My mother and many of the lesbians of her generation—especially if they were black women—didn't have the same sense of freedom from most forms of backlash (including potentially being fired or not hired or denied housing) that is available to lesbians today.

Whether we are considering lesbians from earlier generations or from today, it seems naive to question if sexual orientation affects one's financial choices, right? You'd be surprised.

Dr. M. V. Lee Badgett gets to the heart of the matter in her seminal research tome, *Money, Myths, and Change: The Economic Lives of Lesbians and Gay Men*, with the statement: "But from the second our alarm clocks rouse us to start a new day, each moment is full of potential economic significance and is influenced by our gender, ethnic, and sexual identities."[22] The fullness of Dr. Badgett's observation came to light during my interview of Liz, a Latina lesbian who works as an in-house employment lawyer for a major financial services company. She's a long way from the Brooklyn public housing projects where she grew up.

Like all of us, Liz's adult relationship with money and her expectations of it in the context of her romantic relationships have been deeply influenced by her childhood experiences. Today, her income and assets provide the financial security necessary so that she is no longer on edge "waiting for a train wreck," but the vestiges of fear still surface every now and again, though not in the same way or with similar consequences.

Her father was a very generous man, most times to a fault and to the detriment of his wife and three daughters. He had a fifth-grade education, spoke very little English, and worked mostly menial jobs. Because of the work he did, he got paid in cash, and every Friday he'd go drinking with his buddies. He sometimes came home without enough money for groceries for the upcoming week. When this happened, he also came home to an angry wife. According to Liz, "He's the guy who always felt like if he bought people drinks, they would think he was terrific. If we were eating Spam or Vienna sausage and rice, it was because we knew that he had overspent when he was drinking, and we didn't have enough money for quality food."

Living hand to mouth was common in her household. And whenever they split up (her parents split up and got back together five times), her mother would send Liz and her two younger sisters to get money from her father before he spent it, so that she and the girls could survive. I feel like I'm in the room with her when she describes counting the cash they collected from their father and putting it in piles for the various bills like rent and food. When I ask her what kind of imprint this left on her, she responds, "It was terrible. . . . It always felt like the sky was going to fall." Liz and her sisters attended Catholic school all the way through high school. Interestingly, there was always enough money for their tuition even if the family may not have always eaten balanced meals or high-quality food. To this day, she doesn't know how her parents did it.

Given the financial insecurity Liz grew up with, it is understandable that she'd "look for somebody who is capable of taking care of [herself]." In fact, she almost didn't get to a second date with the woman she was ultimately with for ten years. When they met, Liz thought Debbie worked retail, because Debbie mentioned having to work on a Saturday. To Liz that meant Debbie must have a low-paying retail job, and Liz wasn't interested. As it turns out, Debbie was the director of a program with a social services agency, and the Saturday work was related to an event the agency was sponsoring. Debbie was a highly educated (she has a master's degree), low-earning professional, and she owned her apartment. This combination sat much better with Liz. It meant she wouldn't have to be a caretaker, a role she seemed to always find herself in in her relationships and with her sisters. It also meant she wouldn't always be the one who earned a higher salary—at least there was "the potential [for Debbie] to make a good living."

And as time moved on, her girlfriend did get different, higher-paying jobs. When they broke up, Debbie was working as a full-time therapist in private practice and as an adjunct professor. Likewise for Liz: over the course of their relationship, she completed college (she went back at twenty-eight) while working full-time and then graduated from law school.

Money was an issue at various times throughout their relationship during the years they lived together. Ironically, those tough times became more pronounced as Liz and Debbie's incomes increased! They lived in the apartment Debbie owned, but as Liz's salary as a lawyer increased she began to assume more and more of the household expenses. Liz didn't mind, because there once was a time when she was struggling and Debbie "picked up some of the slack during that time." Not only did her increased salary go to pay more of the household's bills, but she also made a sizeable contribution to Debbie's tuition for the additional schooling she needed for her psychoanalytic training.

Although Liz's income covered most of the bills, she was comfortable with their arrangement of having Debbie handle paying the bills. However, what she did not appreciate was being "put on an allowance," even if it was meant to curb her loose, impulsive spending habit (a trait she had picked up from her father). Liz began to resent the allowance, and while she didn't mind financially contributing to Debbie's education, she also began to resent how much of it she was underwriting. She was making more money than she could have ever imagined, and she was feeling deprived of enjoying the benefits!

Thankfully, Liz possesses a high degree of self-awareness, so she recognizes she ceded control of her money to Debbie. She did it for the same reasons many of us make similar choices, and not just regarding money matters—it was easier to cede control than to have a potentially thorny discussion about boundaries. But there's another reason it was easier not to talk about it, and this reason is common for people who have grown up living hand to mouth and are now making a living where they don't have to worry about how the "mortgage is going to get paid or how they are going to eat or what they'll be able to eat." Liz hadn't sufficiently dealt with her financial insecurity. When you grow up waiting for the next financial train wreck to come, it can take a while to let the feeling of financial safety enfold you and to allow the reality that you are financially safe catch up with your sizeable and healthy income statement and balance sheet.

Liz also has an underdeveloped ability to let others express their generosity. This, too, is something that is left over from growing up in a financially insecure household. We saw Liz's generosity with Debbie, and she also exhibits it with her sisters, especially her sister who is developmentally delayed. And she is munificent with her friends. She is great at giving but admittedly sucks at receiving. Her friends have made comments like: "We want to buy you a beer or dinner sometimes, too." "We have good jobs too, you know." "Why don't you just let somebody do something nice for you?" She grew up in a family where her father was always borrowing, and she saw people bailing him out. It is hard for her to see someone's gesture to buy her a gift or treat her to a beer and dinner purely as their own expression of generosity and love and not as something she has to pay back. Liz is working on opening up to be a better receiver and to appreciate that others' acts of kindness and her ability to take care of herself can coexist.

The Party Is Over

Jody

"I do. There are perhaps no two smaller words that wield so much power over the way people live. But when you marry, there's more that intertwines than just hearts and souls. You wed attitudes and biases toward saving, spending, and planning for the future," says Gayle B. Ronan in her article "For Love and Money."[23]

When Jody and Mike got married, they weren't aware of Nicholas H. Wolfinger's study or his subsequent book, *Understanding the Divorce Cycle: The Children of Divorce in Their Own Marriages*. In both the study and book, Wolfinger, an assistant professor in the University of Utah's Department of Family and Consumer Studies, states, "Growing up in a divorced family greatly increases the chances of ending one's own marriage, a phenomenon called the divorce cycle or the intergenerational transmission of divorce." What they knew, according to Jody, is that neither of them "[had] seen marriage done properly. . . . Both our parents are divorced, and we each have a brother that's divorced."

Jody and Mike were committed to their marriage lasting and, like many engaged couples, entered premarital counseling to ensure its success. So when Jody walked down the aisle, she did it with the full intent and presumption that her marriage would truly be "till death do us part." Yet seven years later, she finds herself newly separated and en route to a divorce. Instead of planning for children, she is in the midst of untangling all that has been entwined and facing the unimaginable prospect of making a one-time, six-figure payment to her husband.

The American Academy of Matrimonial Lawyers, specialists in family law since 1962, list the following, in order of prevalence, as the most common reasons why marriages fail:

- poor communication
- financial problems
- a lack of commitment to the marriage
- a dramatic change in priorities
- infidelity
- failed expectations or unmet needs
- addictions and substance abuse
- physical, sexual, or emotional abuse
- lack of conflict resolution skills

On this list, "financial problems" is noted as the number two reason for marital discord; it was the number one reason for the disharmony in Jody and Mike's household. And it was a topic *not* covered in their premarital counseling sessions.

Why didn't their counselor include discussions about money in their sessions? Why weren't they encouraged to fully disclose their respective financial situations? We'll never know; however the mystery is further complicated by the fact that their counselor was Jody's pastor and Mike's friend and the one who had introduced the two of them. But let's put the counselor's negligence aside for a moment. Jody didn't think to ask Mike about his financial situation. Even though she was completely transparent about hers, she didn't think she was entitled to pry into his. "It never occurred to me that he was lying. It never occurred to me that he was withholding information. It did occur to me not to ask questions because that would insult him."

Jody's story is a cautionary tale of misplaced trust, emotional risks not taken, and the financial cost of shying away from hard conversations with Mike and, maybe more importantly, with herself.

Jody is a self-described hyper-responsible person and has been since she was a young child. "I was the type of kid who, you know, saved her birthday money until Christmas. . . . I loved saving money, and I was very careful about what I bought because I wanted special things. I was never one who just went out and bought impulsively." Her financial habits and beliefs—as is the case with all of us—are in direct response to her upbringing. We either choose to replicate what we witnessed growing up or to do the opposite. Sometimes this choice is conscious; at other times, it is on a subconscious level. For Jody, it was a conscious decision to do the exact opposite of what she saw growing up. "We didn't have a lot of money. . . . Whenever there was a crisis, a car repair or an emergency, I remember my father having a fit like [it] was a financial catastrophe." She vowed she'd never be in that position. She would always live within her means and have money so that nothing would "freak [her] out." And she always has.

Her tendency to save and be purposeful about what she spent money on is how she has been able to live well regardless of the size of her paycheck. She made it a point to save whether she earned a lot—when she worked in high-tech sales—or a little (comparatively speaking) as in her current position as an assistant college provost. Her discipline is the reason she was able to switch careers and work in an industry she loves, even though it isn't as lucrative. It is also what enabled her to purchase an apartment in a tony section of New York City at a young age.

Jody had the impression Mike was also good with money; she saw him as a "very successful guy." After all, he owned a business and wined and dined her while they were dating, taking her to fancy restaurants and spending several hundred dollars each time. He must be doing well, right?

But looking back, Jody says the signs of financial strife were there from the beginning, starting with the fact that "[Mike] didn't have money to help plan [their] wedding." According to Jody, Mike, who is a self-employed consultant, said he couldn't contribute because money was tight due to the bad economy and fewer clients than usual. She presumed his business was simply going through a slow period. Having worked in sales herself, she was familiar with the cyclicality of business, in general, and sales, in particular, so she could empathize and wasn't alarmed.

The first glimpse into the seriousness of Mike's financial problems came a little over six months into their marriage, when they filed their taxes. Mike had taken money out of his retirement account to sustain his lifestyle. He did this at the beginning of the year in which they got married. Therefore, the consequences didn't just affect him. Mike's early withdrawal, which was unbeknownst to Jody, resulted in them having to pay a big penalty the first year they filed joint taxes.

She continued to learn things she wished she had known beforehand. For example, she knew he had student loans (they had both attended the same Ivy League university for graduate school), but she thought the amount was manageable since he'd been out of school for a while and was presumably paying it off; she had no idea it was $80,000. And she had no clue he was about to default on those student loans and had maxed out his credit cards.

Jody discovered what she now refers to as his financial deception before they even celebrated their first anniversary. But before reaching this point, she really felt "he was ashamed of these things. . . . He was really embarrassed about this and couldn't bear telling me." At the time, this posture made sense to her. "I really had no idea that he was in such bad financial [straits] because he wined and dined me. I mean, you don't go out for hundred-dollar dinners if you're broke. I also thought he had some money saved up." She mistakenly projected her good financial habits onto Mike.

Armed with one part empathy, one part sympathy, and one part determination to not let money tear her marriage apart, she went about creating a game plan for paying off Mike's debt. It was a tough time, but within three years, his credit card debts were paid in full, and they had refinanced his student loans to a very low amount and made a huge dent in the balance. Plus, when she learned that his business wasn't really just going through a slow period, it was on life support (there were two six-month periods where he didn't have any paying clients), she helped him get it back on track.

Along the way, though, something happened within her and between them that another round of counseling couldn't fix. Jody began to feel less like a wife and more like a mother—in large measure because of how he responded to her efforts to keep them in the black financially. What she viewed as being responsible and disciplined, he viewed as her nagging and being controlling. Their fights about everything, including money, escalated, and Mike became "verbally abusive" with Jody. He started blaming her for all that was wrong in their marriage.

To talk about marriage these days, it seems, is to also talk about divorce. When referring to the state of American marriages, whether in print or on television, an oft-quoted (though disputed) statistic is that half of all marriages end in divorce. "[The one in two] figure is based on a simple—and flawed— calculation: the annual marriage rate per 1,000 people compared with the annual divorce rate. But some researchers say that this is misleading because the people who are divorcing in any given year are not the same as those who are marrying," says Dan Hurley in the article, "Divorce Rate: It's Not as High as You Think."[24] You might say that the disagreement among social scientists is nothing more than the splitting of hairs; after all, if you are the one going through the divorce, it is really irrelevant whether the statistic is 50 percent or 41 percent (the number social scientists prefer). The only number that matters is a whole number, not a percentage, and it is two: you and your soon-to-be ex-spouse.

Having reached her saturation point emotionally and financially, Jody asked Mike for a divorce. He's now fighting with her about the apartment she bought before they married, claiming rights, which in New York State he legally has, to the apartment's appreciation and increased market value. So, there is a strong possibility she is going to have to make a one-time payment of six figures as part of their divorce settlement. Not quite spousal support, but damn near close!

It'd be easy to blame money for their pending divorce, but it wasn't about money in and of itself—it never is. Money is a mirror that magnifies what is or isn't working in a relationship. For Jody and Mike, it highlighted insurmountable, noncomplementary differences about philosophy, habits, discipline, and character.

Sarah

I am acutely aware that many aspects of my lifestyle wouldn't be possible were it not for the sacrifices of the women (and men) who participated in the women's movement of the 1960s and '70s—also known as Second Wave feminism. Their efforts, along with those involved with the civil rights movement, paved the way for many of the freedoms my generation takes for granted. It is not because we are an ungrateful brood but because living with these rights is all we have ever known. I can't imagine not having the ability to get a credit card in my own name, control over my reproductive health and well-being, the right to vote, or the choice to work and have a family. These are but a few of the issues the women's and civil rights movements of forty years ago addressed, and collectively they combine to give my peers and me unparalleled independence to design lives of our own creation.

Singularly defining the women's movement, whether you are referring to the First Wave (pre-1960s), Second Wave, or Third Wave (post-1980), is difficult and futile. For starters, there are many different types of feminism within each wave, and each has its own philosophy, focus, and corresponding movement. Additionally, feminism is expressed and experienced in diverse ways within waves as well as across waves.

Coming up with a unified definition of feminism or what it means to be a feminist may be pointless, but I believe it is safe to say that a critical element of the women's movement was to help society at large move away from a common "social misconception that all women who work did so to supplement men's wages."[25] This shift in perspective was sorely needed in order to foster financial independence for women, an initiative that continues today.

However, what I find striking about the women's movement and its efforts to empower women to be financially independent is the lack of emphasis on financial interdependence. Too much dependence is bad, but so is too little. And if you as a strong, financially savvy, and independent woman find yourself with a man who is less skillful with money and quite indifferent to it to boot, what do you do?

"I think the hardest thing is that it's not just that the person without the money [or] the person that's bad with money needs skills on how to get better with money, it's just that the person who's good with money needs skills [on] how to work with their partner on how to get them up to speed," Sarah said, as we were winding down our interview. And then she asked, "How do you do this without infantilizing the other person?" It is a profound question and one that comes from deep within a person who has first-hand experience struggling with how to find a balance between financial independence and financial interdependence, especially when too much of either comes at an emotional cost. Her question is reminiscent of a great line from the 1997 movie *Love Jones*, which is equally thoughtful and apropos: "Everyone talks about getting married. I wish someone would tell you how to stay married."

Sarah is still in love with her husband, even though they've been divorced for a year. They were together for close to seven years, two of which she describes as blissful. But try as they might, even with marriage counseling, they couldn't close the gulf that had slowly been developing between them.

Money alone wasn't the reason their relationship ended; however, it cast a spotlight on the myriad issues they were confronting, and prompted them to reexamine the nature of their relationship. After a while, they each had to face a painful fact: you can no longer lie to yourself, and by extension to your mate, about what's working and what isn't.

Sarah and Phillip had a whirlwind romance and eloped before either knew anything about the other's financial situation or proclivities. Soon after their marriage, though, she realized how different their money styles were—and not only was he in debt, but he had no clue how much debt he was in. In some respects the financial dynamics in Sarah and Phillip's marriage were in stark contrast to those of her parents, and in other ways they were eerily similar.

Sarah grew up in the upper-middle class. Both her parents are from Germany and come from families that lost their wealth during World War II and rebuilt it the United States. Her dad was the breadwinner, and her mom was a stay-at-home mom who did a lot of volunteer work at school and the Episcopalian church the family attended. As she describes him, "Dad is very logical, very linear, very discipline[d], very rigid, very good with money and conservative with money." Her mom, on the other hand, is a "binge spender; she's kind of loopy-lou with her money." I chuckle when she tells me, "Mom always complained that Dad wouldn't let her have a maid; he wouldn't let [Sarah and her sisters] take horseback riding lessons or attend private schools." Though they had the money to do all these things and more, he just felt these were "too pretentious," and he didn't want his children growing up as "snobs." Her mother couldn't disagree more; to her, these were things families with their financial means did. In terms of financial practices and philosophy, her parents were polar opposites. Shortly into her marriage to Phillip, she'd discover that they, too, were polar opposites when it came to practices and philosophy.

Her parents were major patrons of the arts, and Sarah's inherited love for the arts morphed into a love of artists. She has only ever dated artists, and naturally, Phillip was one as well. Soon into their marriage, she learned that he was barely paying his bills, didn't know he was $40,000 in debt, and owed years of back taxes. She became overwhelmed and felt responsible for helping him pay these off, especially since she wanted him to be in good standing when they applied for a mortgage. So she sold some of her personal stock to help him pay down his credit card and tax debts.

Phillip is the stereotypical "starving" artist; he is excellent at his craft (he's a musician) but not very good at handling the business side. Case in point: he'd go on tour but would never run the numbers to make certain he was making a profit, or at least breaking even. Sarah would get frustrated because he didn't (or wouldn't) recognize that it cost him (and thus them) money to do his art. She says, "I couldn't get him to [put together] a budget where he could figure out whether he was making enough on his tour to pay for the tour. He would never do it. I could not get him to do it the whole time we were together."

She not only couldn't get him on a budget for his business, she couldn't get him on a budget for their personal finances either. Even though he was a working artist and earned income, she was always the primary earner during their entire marriage and just kept getting better-paying jobs to compensate for his low, or sometimes nonexistent, income—especially as their expenses increased with the purchase of a house in the Bay Area that she loved and he felt burdened by. Eventually this pattern wore her out physically, emotionally, and psychically. She reached the conclusion that "not only was he eating up more of the finances, he wasn't being responsible." It created a lot of stress for her; she tired of "trying to control someone else's behavior, which is neither an easy or realistic thing to do."

Interestingly, the stress revealed something to Sarah that surprised her. "Ultimately, when I got into the relationship and my head got out of the clouds, I had to come down to the reality that one of the things that I want is something that's more in line with what I got from my dad, which is stability around money." She further disclosed, "I do think that I struggle, [particularly] since I'm a very independent woman, with trying to identify myself. Am I really truly independent, or do I just want another daddy to take care of me, you know? Someone like my father who I completely trust with money." Sarah's transparency is worth noting because not too many women disclose this sort of inner struggle with such candor. She comes to the conclusion, the more we talk, that she's not really looking so much for someone to take care of her as she is someone who can be on equal footing with her financially.

In a short span of time, we have gone from the idea that all women who work do so to supplement men's wages to the cultural reality that a growing number of women out-earn their husbands. And many of these women are seeking men who are their financial equals, if not in earning power then at least in terms of fiscal awareness and responsibility. Alana Wingfoot gives us another way of looking at this shift in her 1998 blog post, "Different Generations, Different Issues." She posits the following as what distinguishes the Second Wave from the Third when it comes to women's financial concerns:

> getting paid work, even if you're married or a mother vs. getting better paid work, so we can support ourselves and our family;

> getting women into positions of political power vs. getting women into positions of economic power;

> making it acceptable for mothers to work vs. earning enough money so we can afford to become mothers.

Sarah's challenge, as with many of the issues you and I face (or may potentially face) in terms of love and money, is almost out of the realm of possibility when viewed from the perspective of our mothers' generation. And it reminds me that sometimes you have to pass the baton to yourself—some wisdom has to be attained from direct and sometimes painful experience.

Sarah isn't sure she'll marry again. But she has started to date, and this time around she's vowed to ask the uncomfortable questions, ask them early, and then watch for consistency. She now realizes that asking a man if he's good with money may seem unromantic, but it is actually one of the most loving questions you could ask of the person whose financial life may become entangled with yours. Is it touchy? Yes! Is it loaded? Absolutely! It may seem as if you are asking a simple yes or no question, when in fact you are asking if the person pays their bills on time, if they believe in retirement planning, and how they manage financial challenges. Is it intrusive? Not if you're the one who is good with money and are looking for clues on how to bring your mate up to speed in a way that honors both of you. Not if having a healthy relationship with your mate includes finding a balance between financial independence and financial interdependence.

Kirsten

After having undergone significant changes, divorce laws in the last forty years are much less constricting. Consequently, the process of getting out of a marriage—whether here in the United States or across the pond in Europe—has been rendered *relatively* easy. Dissolving a marriage has become so prevalent it is hard to imagine there once was a time when divorce was actually illegal, except under the most severe of circumstances. (In fact, "divorce was banned in Italy, Spain, and Ireland until 1970, 1980 and 1996, respectively."[26]) Today, divorce is so common that even if you take into consideration the misleading and sometimes conflicting divorce statistics, we have reached a point in our society where "more marriages end due to divorce than to [the] death" of a spouse.[27]

As the divorce laws changed on both sides of the Atlantic, so did the divorce rates. "The rise in divorce rates has been very pronounced in Europe since the 1960s. Virtually all European countries experienced less than 2.5 divorces per 1,000 married people in 1960, and many had divorce rates below 1; by 2002, the divorce rate increased to 5 per 1,000 married people or higher."[28] In comparison, the U.S. divorce rate per 1,000 married people was 2.2 for 1960 and 3.8 in 2003.[29] Whereas Europe experienced a spike in its divorce rate fairly recently, America's spike occurred in the late 1970s and early 1980s.[30] Ironically, when divorce was on the rise thirty to forty years ago, there was still a social stigma associated with being divorced. Nowadays, divorce is seen as more acceptable, yet the trend is on a steady decline in both the United States and Europe.

Cultural diffusion probably best explains the almost lock-step pattern of the divorce trends in the United States and Europe. Which is why, with social and cultural shifts that tend to materialize in tandem, it is not too surprising to discover that two people who grew up approximately 5,500 miles apart were exposed to similar expectations of family structure.

Kirsten and Jay, both born in the 1970s, she in the United States and he in the United Kingdom, came of age during a time of tremendous social and cultural upheaval in their respective countries. While the parents of many in their peer group were divorcing in the midst of these changes, theirs remained and still are married. Kirsten and Jay grew up with the world giving them the message "Divorce is permissible," while closer to home the message was "Stay married through the inevitable ups and downs of a marriage." If it weren't for the research findings of social scientists, this dichotomy wouldn't be so striking.

Thus it is only natural to surmise the opposite: the marriage of offspring whose parents stayed married should likewise remain intact.

Kirsten graduated college in 1989 and accepted a job that required her to relocate. At twenty-two, she moved sight unseen to London, five time zones away from her family, friends, and country of origin! Her employer, one of the world's largest fashion retailers, set her up in a hotel for all of two weeks. She then spent the next six months living in a youth hostel that "was not very nice" until she found a flat of her own.

Moving as she did and when she did was certainly a gutsy move. But for Kirsten's family, making plucky decisions seems to be intergenerational. Her parents immigrated to the United States from Germany during World War II as young adults. They each came to America with nothing more than a desire along with a drive not to end up poor in a foreign country—they could not imagine a more hellish prospect.

After her parents met and married, they started what over the years would become a very successful travel agency. Her mother often did the books for the office at home using ledgers, and Kirsten helped out by organizing the checks. This seemingly small task exposed Kirsten to a necessary fundamental for running a business and, ultimately, a life—how to manage debits and credits. And though it was her mother who invested the family's assets in the real estate and stock markets, it was her father who taught Kirsten and her brother how to read the *Wall Street Journal*. He even had them "invest" in the stock market with pretend portfolios. Aside from the investing tutorials and helping out with some of the family business's administrative tasks, money, paradoxically, wasn't actually talked about in their household, according to Kirsten. Nonetheless, these sessions, coupled with what she observed, fostered in her a keen sense of business and a natural inkling for managing her own money—as well as multimillion-dollar divisions for her employer.

It is said that opposites attract, and from the beginning, Kirsten and Jay were opposites when it came to their philosophies about money and their approaches to financial matters. She came to their relationship with money of her own and a proclivity to save and invest, a college education, professional experience with a multinational company, and an aversion to credit card debt. He, on the other hand, walked into it without a college education, a propensity to spend all that he earned, experience working mostly in small businesses, and $10,000 in debt. At first the disparity in their financial backgrounds was not a concern for Kirsten. She happily took on the task of "teaching him how to get out of debt."

But eventually it did become an issue. Thinking the problem was purely financial, they decided that she'd continue "doing the corporate thing" while he "developed businesses and invested in real estate." The plan was that she'd quit her corporate job and join him in running the various ventures once Jay was able to generate sufficient revenue and cash flow to replace her hefty income. Unfortunately, his results did not reflect his zeal. He got one real estate deal off the ground, but none of the other projects were materializing; in fact, they were losing money, and a lot of it. Instead of taking the losses and moving on, Kirsten used her personal money to make the business whole before they ultimately closed it down. Her choice had far-reaching ramifications for both of them. She says, "I don't know what damage it did to the relationship that I paid off what he felt was his [via the business] debt."

What threw Kirsten and Jay's marriage into a tailspin was his affair, from which they were not able to recover. When she decided to divorce her husband of eight years, she also quit her job, made plans to travel the world for two years, and decided to relocate back to the United States. I interviewed Kirsten three-quarters of the way into her two-year hiatus, just as her divorce was becoming final. She sounds like someone who has recently spent a lot of time reflecting on her choices and the lessons she has learned. She is giving everything she has, and then some, to rebuilding her life.

Only someone who has spent time on a journey of self-discovery could take a hard look at her choices and have the courage to see that the other side of a strength of hers was her Achilles' heel as well. It is a classic misunderstanding: she mistook the control she had from managing financial matters with precision as being in control of her life and someone else's. The subtle distinction became glaringly obvious to her when she realized, "[I married] someone [who] was not my equal [because] I was trying to control life."

"Control" is tricky for many if not all of us. It can reward you on one hand and just as easily penalize you on the other. Likewise, it can prevent you from seeing in the moment what is *so obvious* through the prism of a rearview mirror. For example, Kirsten says if "the affair [had] not happened I think we may have still been together, even though it would not have been the right thing for me or for him." And noticing when you've crossed that *thin line* marking the subtle distinction between being controlling and having control is usually only discernible, as in Kirsten's case, in hindsight. Even she admits that "letting go of corporate life, selling the house, selling the car, putting my stuff into storage, and just traveling and not worrying about my money for two years and just spending based on what I wanted to do was almost a reaction to how I was trying to control life before." She continues, "I mean, in some ways you could say the way I handled my finances was also a control on my finances. You know, I would rather save than have spent it on something."

Learning how to identify the line before it becomes a problem is a skill Kirsten is honing. It is requiring that she redefine some things about herself, in particular, and life, in general. She is discovering how to be comfortable with no specific conclusions, how to sit with ease with questions that cannot be easily or quickly answered, and how to accept the likelihood that when the picture she wants doesn't match the one she has, it just might be a good thing.

As I say every chance I get, money is never just about money. Yet, it is always self-revelatory.

Death Always Comes Too Soon

Toni

Sad but true: none of us are exempt from mortality. Sadder still is the fact that we never know "the day or the hour." Some of us will die after a long battle with an illness; others will die unexpectedly. In either case, the death of a spouse is the second leading reason for the dissolution of a marriage.

As much as I know death is a fact of life, it is not one I easily embrace. Yet in an interesting twist of fate, I might not have been inspired to create the "Women, Money, and Romance" workshop that preceded this book or to write this book itself were it not for the questions death prompted me to ask. Just as we have a tendency not to talk about money substantively, we also tend to shy away from having similar conversations about death.

Yet, the relationship between death, grief, and money is almost inextricable when it comes to the death of a spouse or significant other with whom your finances are entwined. And one of the things I think is unbelievably unfair about life is that it asks you to make decisions that can potentially have far-reaching consequences while you are in an altered state. I have observed how a widow's grieving process can be interrupted by the discovery of what is unknown or partially known as she goes about making these important decisions.

On February 6, 2003, I was struck with a deep, piercing pain I had never experienced before. This was the day Deno, a dear friend who was like an older brother, died of a brain aneurysm; it was two days after his forty-first birthday.

He was too young for the arms of death to touch him; his wife, Marcie, my college roommate, was too young to be a widow; and their daughter was too young to be without a father who adored her.

Deno and Marcie were together for nineteen years, and during their entire marriage they never commingled their assets. His sudden death brought to light just how little she knew about his finances, particularly his investments.

A month after Deno passed away, the father of my friend Annette died. Though he had been battling an illness for several years, his death was still a surprise. However, a bigger surprise awaited my friend's mother, who had been married to her husband for almost forty years. Unbeknownst to her, her husband had accumulated $500,000 in debt. To avoid being obligated for this debt and to protect what assets she could, she declared bankruptcy.

It has been ten years since Toni lost her husband, Jim, to cancer. Like Marcie, Toni was also widowed at a young age, thirty-eight, making them, according to the Census Bureau's statistics as of 2003, two of the 4.2 million women who lost their spouses before the age of forty-five. It is common knowledge that women generally outlive their husbands, but I was surprised at how many women are widowed at such a young age. I want to write about Toni's story because it perfectly illustrates how young widows, in particular, are likely to travel through several marital statuses before they leave their forties. Along the way, each must rethink how she managed money in her first marriage, how she manages money as a widow, and how she is likely to manage money in her next marriage. For Toni, she says of having been single, married, widowed, engaged, and now single again, "It's taught me to be more aware, more knowledgeable, more in control, and to never, ever give up that control."

She and Jim got married in the mid-1980s when Toni was twenty-eight and Jim was forty-seven. Jim was a retired undercover cop whose earnings came from his pension and a part-time job he took to occupy his days. Toni was on the fast track, climbing the corporate ladder en route to her current role as a senior human resources professional. The difference in their ages was just as drastic as the difference in their earnings. The former was never a problem; the latter was occasionally, but only when she "would inwardly wish it weren't so very lopsided." But it was something she'd "never raise because there was nothing he could do about it. . . . It seemed to be an unfair sword to wield around."

In their eleven years of marriage, Toni can recall two or three incidents when they had a "strong disagreement about how to spend." Aside from these rare occasions, they were usually in sync. And since it was the go-go '80s, they spent quite freely—money "was flowing like milk and honey." Looking back, Toni says she would have reined some of that in during their marriage—she certainly had to after Jim's death. Toni may have been the primary earner, but she, just like a lot of widows, had to reevaluate her spending behavior and make some adjustments. This isn't unusual. Widows tend to become hyper-responsible about the money that comes to them due to their husbands' death; it creates an odd relationship. The money is there to help you with immediate and long-term obligations, but the reason you now have the money (be it from an insurance policy, pension benefits that now come to you, or another source) is because of your spouse's death. And if a woman depended on her husband's salary, the adjustment can be really extreme as she works to adapt to less overall income or replace the income lost.

When I ask Toni what becoming a widow taught her about what she *didn't* know about money in her marriage, aside from "spend less" and "pay down debt," she has an interesting response. She believes she was not sophisticated enough about money at the time of her marriage to play forward the ramifications of some of her choices. She shares two salient examples. Both expose our inability to know what will happen in the future and our limited capacity to know what details will be necessary and what preferences will be important to us.

If you are currently married and own a home with your spouse, was there a provision in your closing paperwork for opting to have the bank pay off the mortgage if you or your spouse should die? Toni remembers looking at the paperwork, seeing this option, and choosing not to take it. Who knew seven years after the closing, Jim would die? Had they chosen the option, the house they bought and shared together would have been immediately paid off, "catapulting [Toni] into another category either in terms of being able to buy the next house or living mortgage-free."

If you are like Toni or a number of the other women profiled in this book and you out-earn your husband or significant other, have you fully thought through what your life will be like given the disparity in your incomes? Toni had not twenty years ago, but it is all she thinks about now. And it is one of the reasons she called off her engagement. She says, "I think I've had to be very realistic about what that number means and translates into and what kind of life we're gong to have, and what kinds of subliminal as well as overt issues will arise when the numbers are so disparate." The disparity didn't cause an emotional wedge between her and Jim (her first husband), but it did with Chris (her ex-fiancé). She describes it as follows: "At forty-nine, there's just so much more to lose at this point." She adds, "I can't start over [financially]." Plus, she says, "It is tough enough to finance [my own] twilight years. . . . If I have to do it for two . . ." She finds this thought absolutely terrifying.

Toni literally and figuratively can't afford to miss opportunities to protect her financial future or to be unsophisticated about the consequences of her choices. And neither can you, especially if children are involved. Thus, it is profoundly important that you prepare yourself for the inevitable and that, likewise, you prepare your mate for the possibility that you may predecease him or her. As unimaginable as the process is, it is one of the greatest acts of love the two of you can give to one another.

What follows is what I call a "love letter." It's more like a checklist prepared to demonstrate your affection for your beloved. Having these documents at the ready and properly completed will go a long way in being able to get through those initial days, weeks, and months when handling financial matters is truly the last thing you want to do.

General Docs

Please note that for some of the items listed, there should be one for your mate and one for you. Also, not everyone will need all of the documents named. Your personal circumstances will dictate which are relevant for you and your mate.

- Tax returns for the last three years, yours, and your spouse's if filed separately
- Current pension statement or current defined-contribution statement (401(k), 403(b), IRA, Roth IRA, SEP-IRA, KEOGH, etc.)
- Current benefits statement
- Mortgage statement
- Property tax statement
- Life insurance policy or policies
- Home/renter's insurance
- Car insurance
- Will, living will, and/or health care proxy (please note: not all states recognize a living will as a health care proxy)
- Trust documents
- Power of attorney, property and personal
- Passport
- Birth and marriage certificates
- Adoption papers, guardian information (for minors)
- If there were previous marriages, copies of the divorce decrees from those marriages

Contact Information

Make a list of the phone numbers and addresses of your financial and health team.

- Accountant
- Lawyer
- Financial planner

- Dentist
- Doctor
- Children's pediatrician

Financial Records

Compile the information for your banking and credit card accounts.

- Banking institution, account holder's full name and account number (PIN and passwords, if appropriate), branch address where bank account was opened and contact, if available
- Credit card holder's full name and account number (PIN and passwords, if appropriate), online access information, expiration dates, and latest interest rates

Additional Notifications

Supply contact information for those who should be notified as applicable.

- Spouse's employer or clients if business owner
- Social Security Administration

I also suggest making a copy of the contents of your wallet. For credit cards, banking debit cards, and health insurance cards, make a copy of both the front and back. All these documents should either be stored in a fireproof box at home or a safe-deposit box. Someone outside the household should know how to access it.

There are some decisions you must make immediately, especially regarding the funeral arrangements and paying off your spouse's credit card bills and other debt obligations. For everything else, take your time! Give yourself six to twelve months, as long as there isn't a tax consequence to the delay. Decisions you can likely delay are what to do with the funds in the various bank accounts, mutual funds, or brokerage accounts. You can even roll over your spouse's retirement plan into your tax-deferred accounts to continue the tax-deferred status and let it sit in cash until you are ready to allocate how it should be invested. The quality of your choices will be much better if you wait until the emotional dust settles a bit and the pain isn't as acute. There is nothing rational about grief, and it is best to avoid making hasty decisions you can't undo. Be gentle with yourself, and take your time.

The pain of losing your mate to death never completely goes away, but it does become less debilitating. Eventually you may reach a point where the prospect of letting someone new into your heart and life seems possible. Young widows who are open to remarriage face unique financial challenges when the time comes to build a new life with someone else. You and your new mate most likely are coming to the table with assets from your previous marriage, and you may have children. You want to do everything you can to embrace your new love *and* protect what you have—both for yourself and for your children. Move forward into your new life, but be particularly mindful of the choices you make in terms of how you merge your finances with your new mate. For specific ideas on what choices to make, see the section "Considering Another Marriage" in the final chapter.

I wrote this chapter with a dual purpose in mind. It will not only help you and your mate address how to navigate making life-altering decisions, but it is also a blueprint for how you can help if a dear friend of yours loses his or her mate. Instead of asking that dreadful question, "What can I do for you?" you can be at the ready with some ideas to help make those initial days, weeks, and months a little easier to get through.

It is my hope that you and your beloved will have a very long, fruitful life together filled with blessings beyond measure and just enough challenges to help you grow. But the time will come when you will have to say good-bye, and when that happens, taking the steps suggested to have your financial house in order is one last loving gesture.

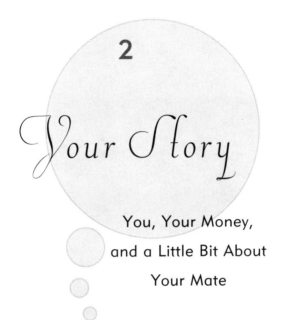

2

Your Story

You, Your Money,
and a Little Bit About
Your Mate

"Revolution begins with the self, in the self."
—**TONI CADE BAMBARA**

Financial Wheel

*M*oney is considered one of America's remaining taboos, and the commonly held perception is that we don't talk about it. I actually disagree with this oft-quoted view; I believe people talk about money all the time. They are just having the wrong conversations, rarely going beyond the superficial to the substantial and significant. The women I interviewed certainly cannot be accused of perpetuating the "don't talk about money" taboo. They opened up to me and thereby to you about matters that are both personal and private, and in so doing enriched us all by sharing their stories.

By peeking into their lives, you were able to see how money shadows every aspect of not only their diverse lives but yours as well. You had an opportunity to examine the interplay of family, society and culture, personal choices, and love, both the love one has and the love one wants, from a distance. Now it is time to come a little closer; it is time to shift the focus to you. The remainder of the book is designed to do just that. It will provide you with a framework for examining the three interconnecting circles of your relationship with yourself, your money, and your mate and how they lead to what you are seeking: financial intimacy.

And I hope you are prepared to work, because that is what financial intimacy requires. You can certainly read this part of the book without doing the exercises, but I suggest you save the passive reading for another book. I guarantee that you won't get as much from this book if you don't actively engage with the exercises. Feel free to write on the pages if pen and paper or a computer is not nearby, especially if that will facilitate the process of you getting to know yourself in a different way—which is what this journey is all about.

Think of the pages that follow as a safe space for reflecting, asking questions, and being led to answers you didn't know you had or needed. It's also important to allow for the very large possibility that some of your questions may go unanswered by the time you finish this book—maybe even indefinitely—and that is OK!

Rarely does a person view money as something with which he or she has a relationship. But you do. And since it is a relationship you carry with you at all times, exploring the relationship you have with money is where are going to begin. First, let's acknowledge a few fundamentals. On the surface, money is really very simple. One plus one will always equal two. Money always flows in two directions—in and out—and it's preferable to have more coming in than going out. It is better to own more than you owe. And, if there is such thing as a magic bullet, it is in the awareness that you create wealth from money working for you, not solely from you working for it. These money tenets have always been and will always be. The *mechanics* of money never change.

The first and only company I worked for before launching my own firm fourteen years ago was a merchant bank. I was twenty years old when I started my career on Wall Street in 1986, four months after graduating college. My mentor hired me to work as an assistant in technology human resources, the only division that supported every profit center in our decentralized company. I could not have been more wet behind the ears, as the saying goes. I knew nothing about stocks and bonds aside from what I had read in the newspaper or seen on the evening news. I went there not knowing what merchant banks do. (They provide trading, investment banking, and investment management services to corporations, governments, large foundations and endowments, and high-net-worth individuals.)

And I had no idea that I would find my calling and fall in love with a profession that was seemingly a far cry from my original aspiration of designing shoes. Nor did I know then that I would be inspired to get my master's in business administration with a concentration in finance, and learn what it takes to start and run a business. (I was part of a team that built a business within the private bank—Private Investment Planning.)

I also had no idea in 1986 how a particular day a year later would shape my sensibilities about money and investing. It is a day I will never forget: Monday, October 19, 1987—otherwise known as Black Monday. It was the day the stock market crashed and set off a worldwide correction. The Dow Jones Industrial Average lost more than five hundred points and experienced the largest one-day percentage decline in stock market history. I don't know if I will ever be able to recount the frenzy of that day in words that adequately describe just how timorous people around me were. The immediate fallout of that chaotic day was widespread, but it didn't take long for a sense of calm to return to the stock market and for it to rally back into positive territory. When it did I learned that the mechanics of money are just one side of the equation. The other and perhaps more unpredictable side of the equation is the *psychology* of money. Black Monday, coupled with my years working in the private bank managing money for high-net-worth individuals, cemented my understanding of how little money actually has to do with money.

Working with money is akin to completing a jigsaw puzzle. The *picture* of what the solved puzzle is supposed to look like is on the outside of the box, and your job is to assemble the disparate *pieces* inside the box such that they resemble the picture. Well, putting the *pieces* together in such a way that you create the *picture* you want is a perfect analogy for what you're going to do as you deepen your understanding of your relationship with money and how that can wiggle itself into the relationship you have with your mate.

The picture consists of the four things you do with money: save, invest, spend, and earn. Whether your income is $25K, $250K, or $2.5Mil, you can only do these four things, and every day you make choices that affect one or any combination of these areas. Each of your daily actions determines both your current financial reality and future financial condition.

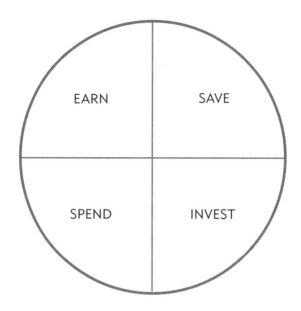

Let's circle the Financial Wheel beginning with the *save* section.

- How much do you want to save in the next thirty days?
- How much do you want to save within the next year?
- What do you want to be able to say you have saved during the course of your lifetime? Why?
- What makes the numbers you have written down important to you?
- Did you give yourself permission to think big, or did you play it safe and write numbers you felt were more realistic? If you did the latter, go back and do it again, this time letting go of any restraints that prevent you from seeing beyond what you believe is possible right now.
- How will you feel if you actually meet your goal at each time interval? How will you feel if you don't?

In moving on to the *invest* section, it's important to keep in mind that this section isn't about how much you want to invest. Instead, you are asked to consider:

- What assets do you want to own?
- Who are the people in your life you want to be able to support, and what causes do you want to be able to help sustain?
- Again, why? What do the assets, people, and causes mean to you?

Have you ever said, "If I had more money, I would (fill in the blank)"? Well, in the *spend* section, consider these questions as if money weren't an issue.

- Where would you go?
- What would you do differently with your time?
- What would you buy?
- What do you envision it would feel like if all this came true for you?
- How would you need to live your life so as to enable what you have written down to manifest?

We round out the Financial Wheel exercise with the *earn* section. There's a reason we conclude this exercise on *earn* rather than one of the other sections, and it will become clear shortly. In the meantime:

- What do you want to earn in the next thirty days?
- How much do you want to earn within the next year?
- What do you want to be able to say you've earned during the course of your lifetime? Why?
- Describe the sense of achievement you anticipate you will feel upon reaching your goals.
- With the numbers you've just written, will you make your target in terms of what you intend to save?
- After you hit your savings target, will there be enough for you to spend it in the ways in which you desire?

Most people have been conditioned to follow a paradigm that advocates designing your life based on what you earn. These same people erroneously confuse this practice with living within your means, which of course you should absolutely do. But by asking you to complete the Financial Wheel starting with *save* and ending with *earn*, I'm submitting for your consideration another approach: *figure out how to earn what you need to lead the life you desire.* One approach is reactive; the other is proactive.

One of the reasons for beginning this journey with the Financial Wheel exercise is to invite you to think about money in all its facets. Far too often, people think and operate with money in a very singular fashion. Sure, on an intellectual level you know you *do* various things with your money, but how often do you consider the fact that each choice you make in one area—save, invest, spend, or earn—has a ripple effect on the other areas, if not immediately, then eventually?

If your Financial Wheel is typical, then you definitely have a gap between *what is* and *what you want.* You haven't saved what you want. You don't own all that you want. You don't have the freedom to spend your money as you'd like, and you are not currently earning what you'd like. Some people get discouraged by the gap. From my perspective, the gap is good. It provides you with clues about new choices you need to make.

I am a firm believer that, if you let it, money can be one of your most invaluable personal development tools. Money will reveal to you where the holes are in your strategy, presuming of course you have one—and if you don't have one, what you need to do to create a strong strategy. It will highlight for you where you need to improve in terms of the discipline you exercise. All of us are extremely disciplined in some areas of life, while simultaneously lacking self-control in others. It can help you refine your discernment skills when making choices. And, finally, money as a personal development tool will show you where you need to be more creative in your thinking.

Several times during the Financial Wheel exercise, the picture portion of the puzzle, you were asked "Why?" Asking why helps you discover the multiple and sometimes conflicting motivations that drive your decisions. It also helps you get behind the numbers to the nonfinancial aspects of your money. Another benefit of *why* questions is that they are a way to segue into the other element of your financial puzzle—the pieces. This is where things get really interesting, because it contextualizes your financial experiences and expectations. You have almost absolute control of your financial picture, but much less control over the pieces. Yet that part of the puzzle has as much, if not more, influence on your experiences and expectations of money.

Pyramid of Wise Money Management

We're going to use this triangle, the Pyramid of Wise Money Management, to fit together the "pieces." Awareness, beliefs, thoughts, and behavior collectively represent the base of the triangle. In the middle section we find reasoning—how do you think things through in general, and how do you arrive at the financial decisions you make? And the tip of the triangle represents purposeful action.

Let's examine each section of the Pyramid, starting at the base.

Awareness, Beliefs, Thoughts, Behavior

- What is your first memory of money, and how has it molded your views about life and money?
- Was there financial peace or discord in your family's household?
- Is money (having it or not having enough of it) a problem for you today, and if so, to what can you attribute the origins of the problem?
- What does money mean to you, and when did you become aware of that meaning?
- To what extent, if at all, do your religious or spiritual beliefs affect how you think about money or what you do with it?
- How do the media and popular culture influence how you view money and the financial choices you make?
- Have you ever had formal personal finance training, or has most of what you learned been through trial and error?

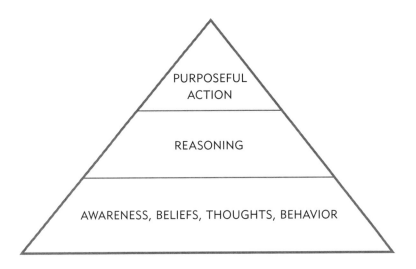

- In what ways has money surfaced as a problem in your love life? How are you handling (or did you handle) it?
- What do you want money to do for you now and in the future?
- What is important to you about money?

Reasoning

Now, let's move up to middle section.

- Are you linear or more abstract in the way you think and the way in which you arrive at decisions?
- As you examine past decisions, would you say you arrived at most of them by being deliberate, or were they accidental, "seat of the pants" types of choices?
- Do you need others to buy into your decision before you feel you've made the right one? If so, who are those others, and why are their opinions so important to you?

You probably think each time you reach into your wallet for your cash, use your credit or debit card, or go online to make a financial transaction that you are simply participating in a monetary exchange. Far from it! Whatever your answers to the above questions are, know that those answers influence you greatly. Your answers color your perspective about money, and your relationship with money, and shadow over every financial decision and choice you make. They also silently influence what you are looking for in terms of love and money.

The base plus the middle section are what lead to the tip of the Pyramid—*purposeful action.* Financial self-awareness is rooted in the three sections that comprise the Pyramid of Wise Money Management and it is what enables you to—more often than not—make choices, in general, and financial ones, in particular, *by design* rather than by default.

You've only just begun your journey, but these two exercises—the Financial Wheel and the Pyramid of Wise Money Management—are critical to understanding the *real* relationship you have with money, past and present, as opposed to the one you believe you have. It is also the springboard from which you can create the relationship you want to have with money in the future.

Financial Modes

*B*ut understanding your relationship with money is not complete without an examination of the way in which you operate with money and how this influences the financial mode to which you belong. There are four modes; which one are you in consistently?

Survive

This mode is best characterized by the person who lives paycheck to paycheck, but barely. When she deposits a check, she does so hoping with bated breath that it clears before any outstanding checks bounce.

Maintain

In the maintain mode, a person has graduated from living paycheck to paycheck but finds it extremely difficult to save.

Thrive

A person in thrive mode is living significantly above a paycheck-to-paycheck level, saving at least 10 percent of her gross income, and is able to make charitable donations with ease.

Excel

As you can probably gather from the progression, excel is the mode we should all strive for. When a person reaches excel mode, she is doing everything in thrive mode, *plus* she's figured out a way to live in part or entirely from money that is working *for* her! Said another way, she can choose how she works and when, because she has passive income (money working *for* her) coming from other sources such as a business venture or investment and real estate holdings.

I have been working in the financial services industry for twenty-three years, and I have witnessed those who are high earners operate in survival mode and those with modest incomes live comfortably in thrive mode, inching quite nicely toward excel mode. Therefore it is imperative that you don't falsely presume, as I have seen people do, that your mode (or the mode of another) is dictated by the size of your paycheck. Likewise, if you are presently in survive or maintain mode, that's OK—it's only temporary. As you move further into this section, you'll discover a blueprint for actions to take that can help you migrate from the lower end of this spectrum to the upper end regardless of your circumstances. It may take some time, but it is possible!

You know how any negotiation is best entered knowing where you stand before you go into it? You know how it is always best if you've thought things through, as if you won't have a chance to mull it over before you have to announce what you are going to offer or willing to accept? Well, there are always at least two people with whom you are negotiating when it comes to money and matters of the heart: yourself and your mate. Together, the Financial Wheel, the Pyramid of Wise Money Management, and knowing your financial mode prepare you for these negotiations. Doing these exercises will give you the insight you need to know where you stand, what you are bringing to the table, and what you'll be willing to accept from what someone else brings to the table.

If you're dating, it's also helpful to think about what you need in order to feel comfortable revealing your answers to the person you're dating, how you'll know when the timing is right, and how you will know when you are ready to ask these same questions of them without judgment. Additionally, you have to know what your deal-breakers are. Yes, all of this is malleable, but you must have a starting point.

If you are already in a relationship, it's helpful to look at these exercises as a way to get to know your mate again. Don't assume you know how he or she will respond. Similarly, this is a chance to reintroduce yourself to your partner. Let this be an opportunity for the two of you to fully step into the natural mystery of getting to know each other.

The Power of Words

These exercises can give you the courage to be open, transparent, and direct with yourself first and then with someone else. I don't have to tell you how hard this is—talk about feeling exposed! Yet financial intimacy requires a willingness to be vulnerable and the grace to give your mate room to be the same. Similarly, it necessitates that you know what sentiments you associate with words that tap into your perceptions of money, because these are the things that are hanging out in the background, quietly affecting how you feel about yourself, your money, and your mate.

Do you remember the expression "Think long, think wrong"? I want you to consider this phrase as you do the next exercise. Don't think long about your responses; simply write what first enters your mind as you go down the list of thirteen words.

1. Trust
2. Power
3. Happiness
4. Control
5. Security
6. Dependency
7. Independence
8. Success
9. Setback
10. Preference
11. Prejudice
12. Confidence
13. Vulnerability

By no means is the above meant to be an exhaustive list, but using these words as a primer does a sufficient job of helping you tap into what money evokes for you. Are you surprised by any of your responses? How many of your responses are directly tied to money? How many indirectly? When your mate completes the word association exercise, compare your respective responses. Doing so will likely open an area of discussion you've yet to explore, and it will definitely deepen your understanding of each other's perception of money. And perhaps it will enlighten each of you about the source of your viewpoints.

If your mate hasn't done so already, he or she should do the same set of exercises that you've done to this point. For maximum impact, you and your mate should do the exercises separately. But before you come together to share and discuss your respective responses, you should also complete the exercises based on *how you think your mate will respond* to the same questions. This is a fascinating approach because it reveals how much you really know about each other versus how much you assume you know. I suspect you both will be surprised a few times over!

A word of advice: engage in this exchange process with the intent to listen to understand and not to prove anything. Also, don't abandon the process if you or your mate begin to feel anything but connected, accepted, and secure in the midst of this experience. The feeling is natural and will soon pass. Plus, the benefit far outweighs the temporary discomfort.

And if you are dating, answer the questions based on how you'd want your soon-to-be mate to respond. I mean it: Complete the Financial Wheel "for" him or her. Think about what answers would make you feel comfortable if you were discussing the different sections of the Pyramid of Wise Money Management. Of the four financial modes, think about which is ideal, acceptable, or a deal-breaker for you. Yes, this is going to feel odd, but you have enough experience to know a bit about what you want and don't want that it shouldn't be too difficult to do. Besides, doing this will fine-tune your observation skills as you date. You'll be amazed at what your "Spidey senses" will detect as you listen and watch for a connection between what is said and done, and whether there is a consistency between the two, as well as for a connection between what is said and done and what you *want* to be said and done. Admittedly, you may jump to some conclusions about the financial character, style, preferences, and habits of the person you are dating that are not completely informed. For example, you might falsely presume he is a high earner when he is not, or you may falsely presume the reverse. You may falsely presume that because she works in a low-earning profession and doesn't exhibit the trappings of wealth that she is not wealthy. I've only provided a short list of possibilities of how you might misread certain clues. As you date, you'll be able to add to this list from what you discover from your dating experiences.

Additionally, by completing the Financial Wheel and Pyramid of Wise Money Management "for" someone else, you do run the risk of trying to create a "perfect" person who doesn't exist. But trust yourself to know when what you have written down in these areas—in terms of what you are looking for someone else to have, do, be, or want—needs to be modified. You may need to adjust your bar because you are getting feedback from your experiences that it is set unrealistically high. Remember, few people will come to the table with their financial house perfectly in order. (Is yours?) What you want is someone with a plan they are executing with commitment!

Regardless of your starting point, the value of all the work you've done already is priceless. The queries, the contemplation, and the discoveries all lead to tremendous self-knowledge that will make you financially stronger, more confident, healthier, and sexier. Yes, sexier! Believe me, when your finances are in order or you're working on a game plan to get them there, your carriage is much different than when they are not.

The Role and Influence of Family

Family and family dynamics have a potent hold on all of us, especially when it comes to money. Issues of power and dominance often surface in the realm of money—regardless of the family's socioeconomic standing. Attitudes, values, and habits, in general, and those concerning money, in particular, are passed down in much the same way as family traditions. And like traditions, the attitudes, values, and habits you inherit tend to inform what you expect from yourself and, therefore, what you will expect from someone else. The purpose of the next set of questions is simple: to place those expectations on the table for constructive contemplation and discussion.

- Did you grow up with both parents or a single parent?
- If single, did your parents divorce, were they never married, or did you lose a parent to an early death?
- If your parents divorced, did either of them remarry?
- If you grew up with both (even if one was a stepparent), did your mother and father work, or just your father or just your mother?
- What type of work did they do? Where did they work?
- Did you grow up with your biological family, with an adopted family, or in foster care?
- Do you have siblings? If so, where are you in the birth order?
- How does your first memory of money compare to your siblings' first memories?
- As adults, how do you and your siblings compare and contrast when it comes to the way in which you handle money today?
- Which parent paid the bills?

- Which parent seemed to be the one making the financial decisions for the household?
- Did your parents save? Did they invest?
- Did they pass down the discipline of saving? Did they teach you about investing?
- In terms of your beliefs about money and how you handle it, do you favor one parent or do you take after both of them?
- Was money talked about constructively in your household? Or was it primarily a source of fights between your parents?
- If your parents fought about money, did they do so occasionally, or were their fights frequent and ongoing?
- Did you grow up in an urban, suburban, or rural environment?
- Did your family live in a house or apartment? Was it owned or rented?
- Did your family take vacations during the school breaks?
- Did you work during the summers of high school and college?
- Did your parents pay for college in part or in full?

Today, you are either continuing the legacy set forth by your parents, thinking you are doing the opposite but really doing the same thing, just differently, or truly doing the complete opposite of them. We needed to revisit your family background, because your financial intimacy training actually started when you were young. More than likely, you have refined your relationship management and communication skills over the years, but the foundation from which you are working stems from your family background and your upbringing. And guess what? The same applies for the person you are dating, living with, married to, or maybe even in the middle of divorcing.

Did you struggle with the more in-depth family background questions? Name some of the emotions that came up for you. While unearthing old family stuff can be cathartic, it is not always a pleasant experience. Often, it is extremely painful. Keep that in mind, because there's a high probability that your mate will also have an unsettling time with this part of the process.

And that is something else to be mindful of: all of this is a *process*! Financial intimacy doesn't happen in the context of a single conversation but over the course of many. Why state the obvious? Because we live in such a performance-driven society, it is often easy to lose sight of this precious fact. Yes, financial intimacy is the outcome you want, but it requires time, effort, and attention to the seemingly small details. Plus, it can't be rushed if it is to evolve organically and be authentic.

The Prince Charming Effect

We needed to revisit your family background for another reason, to bring up what some women find to be a delicate topic: the Prince Charming Effect. Are you familiar with this phrase and what it means? It is used to describe a woman who is educated, financially independent, and able to take care of herself, yet who wants to be taken care of in the classic sense of her husband or partner out-earning her. The Prince Charming Effect taps into the age-old "hunter and gatherer" notion, and most women either embrace or reject it based on what they witnessed growing up.

Are you a hunter or a gatherer? Is your answer by default or because that is your true nature? Do you want your mate to be a hunter or a gatherer? And if what you want him or her to be is different than what he or she is, have you made peace with that? If not, what can you do to come to terms with this reality? As our society moves deeper into the twenty-first century, the trends of dual-income households and women earning more than their husbands are likely to continue to increase, rather than diminish. Therefore, honestly asking and answering this question (remember, there is no right or wrong answer, just what is right or wrong *for you*) will help you avoid (or if it is too late for that, understand how to constructively handle) the internal strife that comes from getting involved with someone with whom you can't play the role you want.

Renee learned this the hard way, and had she asked herself the above questions, she and Charles probably wouldn't have lived in a tension-filled household for so long. They most likely would have just gone out on a few good dates and then happily moved on.

Charles made 50 percent less than Renee. He felt they should split the household bills proportionately, rather than equally; she disagreed. Their differing expectations led to numerous fights about money. But they weren't really fighting about money; it was nothing more than the tool that highlighted some important philosophical differences. It masked her anger at him for not being the man—the hunter—she truly wanted.

Renee, as with most women like her who earn more than their mates, wasn't looking to have a relationship with a man just for his money. However, when she looked at her life, she saw fewer lifestyle options, not more, available to her despite her education and having made smart career moves and savvy financial choices on her own. Her perception made already weighty questions feel even heavier. Could her man take care of her and their children if they got married and started a family? What would happen should she lose her job? When would she ever be able to leave her corporate gig to launch her own business? These are all reasonable and valid considerations, because when reality bumps up against a long-held and often unspoken vision of how you want your life to be, friction and unnecessary unhappiness inevitably follow.

Consider just a few more questions on this important topic.

- If you earn significantly more than your mate, do you think the two of you should split bills fifty-fifty or in a proportion commensurate with your respective salaries?
- What if the scenario were reversed and he or she earned more—would you feel the same?
- If you earn significantly more than your mate, what would make you feel secure in the relationship, financially and otherwise?

The Power and Influence of Habits

The Necessary Details

"Where are you going? Where did you come from?" (Judges 19:17)

The thread that connects where you were, where you are now, and where you are going can be found in a powerful but small five-letter word: *habit*. Habits reveal the degree to which you are in touch with your money by knowing what you have, what you tend to do with what you have, and why.

Most people think of habits purely in the context of the things you *do*. However, habits are not just limited to actions; they extend to modes of thinking as well. So as we go through the eighteen habits in the pages that follow, be on the lookout for habits that are not directly connected to actions you have to take or, in some instances, even directly correlated with money. But know that they *all* affect the condition of your finances nonetheless. Also, as you go through the list, if you notice any resistance to just the mere thought of adopting any of the suggested habits, take heed. That resistance can give you a glimpse into the reasons behind the habits you currently follow.

When I was in undergrad, I remember a professor telling the class, "*Preparation prevents piss-poor performance,*" paraphrasing a British army adage. I have never forgotten those words. And it is how I've come to view good habits, especially those that affect the condition of your finances. They set you up to operate at peak performance and help you rebound quickly when life thwarts your best-laid plans. The habits referenced here are provided in that spirit. (A comprehensive listing of the habits may be found in the appendix.)

Habit #1: Track Your Money

To me, this is where it all begins. Can you relate to this scenario? You go the ATM on Sunday and take out $100. By Tuesday morning, you have just $20 in your wallet and only a vague idea of how you spent $80. Now imagine this going on every week for a year; that is potentially $4,680 that has "disappeared." Extrapolate out two years, three years, four years—that's a lot of money unaccounted for!

When I ask coaching clients and workshop attendees if they know how much money they spent last year *and* on what items, an alarming 80 percent reply no. Of the 20 percent that say yes, half only know the amount of what they spent, but not the details behind the numbers.

The cumulative effect of not knowing what you are spending your money on is costly, and not just financially. When you are unable to account for your money, you miss out on the opportunity to make choices that will enable you to treat it well and in turn have it treat you well. Likewise, you miss the chance to see, on paper, if you are spending your money in ways that support your values, goals, and priorities, and to calculate if you are operating at a profit, break-even, or loss. Ultimately, you miss the chance to increase your *financial productivity* and heighten your *financial self-awareness*.

If you are someone who does not track your money, or if you can ballpark the amount but not the details, I ask that for the next thirty days you track *all* of your money. Get a receipt for literally everything you purchase, make note of every bill you pay, and record all sources of your income. You can use pen and paper, a spreadsheet or personal finance software, or any of the workbooks referenced in appendix B. The actual activity of tracking matters much more than the specific tracking tool!

Are you resisting doing this before you've even begun the task? You are not the first, nor would you be the first if you get off to a strong start and then fall off after a few days. Push through the resistance and get back on the proverbial horse if you do fall off. There is so much power in knowing, I mean *really* knowing, where your money is going, as well as where it is coming from. It is paramount for your financial success as an individual, and it becomes especially critical when your finances are merged with another's!

There are myriad benefits to tracking, but the ultimate one is that it reminds you that you don't manage money, really—*you manage choices.* Tracking exposes the choices you are making and whether those choices are furthering or hindering your efforts to have and be more.

Habit #2: Establish and Follow Financial Policies

What's a financial policy, you ask? Think of it in terms of boundaries or predetermined parameters about how you will spend your cash, use your debit and credit cards, or acquire debt. It is important to know what you will say yes or no to *before* you get into a situation requiring a yes-or-no decision. For example, I love shoes. (There's a reason I wanted to be a shoe designer!) But here's my rule: I can spend whatever I want on a pair of shoes, but I must pay cash! I cannot put it on a revolving credit card, not even if I plan to pay it in full before the end of the billing cycle. Rational? For someone else, perhaps not; for me, it is. Policies are highly personal—each person has to devise a set of policies that is appropriate for her. If you don't create your own policies, you run the risk of following, without realizing you are doing so, the policies set by someone else.

Some people commit to only charging what they can pay in full at the end of a billing cycle. Others only use their credit cards in emergencies. Others commit to only acquiring life-purpose debt and avoid lifestyle debt entirely. Some prefer to use their debit cards for 99 percent of their purchases, because it helps them to track the details better. What might some of your policies be?

Habit #3: Save Before You Pay Your Bills

Which of these two scenarios is the better one to follow?

Scenario A: You have committed to saving a certain dollar amount or percentage of your income each time you get paid.

When the money comes in, you set aside the designated amount for saving. When you go to pay your bills, there isn't enough money to pay all of your bills in full.

Scenario B: You have committed to saving a certain dollar amount or percentage of your income each time you get paid. When the money comes in, you pay your bills in full, but there isn't anything left over to save, so you miss your savings target.

Should you save and be late with paying your bills, or should you pay your bills and postpone saving?

If you are like 70 percent of the people to whom I present these two options, you chose Scenario B—and you are wrong! You actually want to follow Scenario A, which seems counter-intuitive. But there is a dangerous trap with Scenario B that people rarely notice; it lulls you into focusing on the short-term at the expense of the long-term. I'm not encouraging you to be irresponsible. You have to live up to your part of the deal and meet your obligations. However, I am asking that you momentarily let go of wanting to *feel* good in the short-run and use the discomfort to serve your best interest in the long-run. Scenario A presents an opportunity for you to do just that! It prompts you to ask questions and examine your behavior with money in a manner that following Scenario B would never bring about. In other words, Scenario A provokes a degree of creative thinking that Scenario B could never induce.

Unfortunately, far too many people subscribe to an "either/or" philosophy; I say, figure out how you can be a "both/and" person. Adopting this paradigm in the realm of money will certainly spill over into other areas of your life as well. Ultimately, you want to save and pay your bills with ease. From the questions and examinations prompted by Scenario A, you might discover you need to supplement your income or that you need to examine your expenses to determine how to reduce them, even if only temporarily, to make that happen. You might uncover an alternative you'd never considered before. Whatever adjustment you discover you need to make, the likelihood that you would have identified it by following Scenario B is slim to none.

Habit #4: Decide What You Are Going to Save in Advance

Did you save at least 10 percent of your gross income last year? Is that asking too much? OK, let's go to the other end of the continuum: did you save $1,000 last year? Ideally, the goal is to save 10 to 20 percent of your gross income (including what you contribute to your retirement accounts). But if that is impossible due to your current circumstances, shoot for at least $2.74 a day, which amounts to $1,000 a year.

How do you save either 10 percent of your gross income or $1,000 a year, something in between these two figures, or something even greater? One way is to automatically contribute to your retirement and savings accounts so that you never see the funds in your checking account. Or, if your earnings schedule is inconsistent in terms of timing, make a commitment to sweep the target dollar amount or percentage manually before you mentally commingle the saving monies with your disposable or discretionary pool of funds.

Whichever method works best for you, automatic or manual, know what you are going to save *before* the money comes in so that it is not an afterthought, and choose to deviate from it only in the event of an emergency.

Habit #5: Give Your Savings a Purpose

We know we should save, but let's face it, many of us don't like to do it. It means having less today, and we don't like delayed gratification. (It's been that way since we were babies!) We want it—whatever it is—now!

A way to reconcile the natural urge to want it now with the wise choice to plant seeds for the future is to give the money you are setting aside a reason for existing. Enter the role of written goals.

Goals are a portrait of the future you are seeking to create, and there is a financial component to 99 percent of the goals you have (or will have). Interestingly, the money to finance your future goals comes from the money you have *now*. To me, goals are like magnets pulling today's money to some point in the future.

It is not enough to simply have goals floating around in your head or listed on a piece of paper as single-line entries on a long to-do list. You must also know a few details about your goals.

- What's the benefit of achieving this goal?
- What's the deadline? By when do you want to be able to say this goal has been achieved?
- What financial resources do you believe you'll need? If you don't know exactly, estimate.
- What could you do daily to help close the gap between now and the goal's deadline?

Answer these questions for each individual goal, and then add up the financial resources so that you have a cumulative number. At a minimum, your savings target from Habit #4 should be this cumulative number.

Here are some additional considerations to keep in mind when it comes to your goals.

- Is there anyone else who will be impacted by the realization of your goal? How about the fact that you've earmarked money for this goal?
- What, if any, are your concerns or fears regarding your goal?
- Imagine three years have passed and you are looking back over those three years to today. What must you do today to start moving in the direction of the future you want?

Habit #6: Tie Your Investment Choices to Your Savings Purpose

Are you seeing the connections? It's like an interlocking circle of your goals, savings, and investments, with you in the center steering everything. Goals need a proper savings strategy, and your savings need a solid investment strategy. It's all entwined, and one weak link jeopardizes the entire circle. One of the biggest mistakes I see people make is to miss the relationship between goals, savings, and investment choices; when they do, they tend to invest injudiciously.

When it comes to investing, it is extremely important to keep in mind that there is never, *ever*, one singular investment approach that makes sense for everyone. Ultimately, it should be tailored to your particular circumstances and preferences. But there are some universal investment guidelines that are invariable regardless of the investment approach used.

Investing is all about the balance sheet, the instrument used to truly measure if your money is working *for* you. It compares what you *own*, also known as *assets*, to what you *owe*, also known as *liabilities*. The goal: to own more than you owe.

What follows is a brief and basic tutorial on managing your balance sheet; it is not the intention of this section (or this book) to provide a comprehensive investing how-to. Rather, it is to lay the groundwork to ensure that you and your mate are not working at cross-purposes when it comes to managing your individual and collective balance sheets. (For helpful resources and more detailed instructions on how to invest, whether as a self-directed investor or with the assistance of a professional investment advisor, consult appendix B.)

Our overview begins on the asset side, with an emphasis on the stock market. An asset is anything that you own that has commercial or exchange value, meaning you can convert it to cash. Though there are four types of assets (tangible and intangible; financial and nonfinancial), for our purposes we will focus on tangible assets of a financial nature.

The most common line items on the asset side of your balance sheet, listed in accordance with their risk/return profile are cash (at the bottom of the spectrum with low risk, low return) followed by bonds, real estate, and stocks (at the top of the spectrum with high risk/high return). Here are some guidelines.

Cash. Hold at least six months of living expenses in a savings account, money market account, or three-month certificate of deposit.

Bonds. A bond is any interest-bearing or discounted government or company security that obligates the issuer to pay the bondholder a specified sum of money, usually at specific intervals, and to repay the principal amount of the loan at maturity. Bonds are also referred to as *fixed income.*

Very broadly, there are four types of bonds: treasuries, mortgage-backed, corporate, and municipal. Treasuries are the safest because the interest and principal payments are guaranteed by the U.S. government.

Individual bonds are preferable to bond funds because individual bonds provide a fixed rate of return and a return on your principal. Bond funds do not. Municipal bonds, which represent the debt obligation of a state or local government entity, get special tax treatment. Therefore, don't hold municipal bonds in your tax-deferred accounts (e.g., 401(k), 403(b), IRA, or Roth IRA).

Real estate. As an investor, you can participate in the real estate market in a variety of ways, either directly or via a real estate investment trust (REIT). A REIT is a real estate mutual fund that invests in a portfolio of real estate. Income-generating real estate may take the form of rental houses, rent-to-own houses, fixer-uppers, land that you have purchased to subdivide and sell, owner-occupied property with additional units for rent, property purchased at auctions, commercial real estate, or real estate speculation. (Special note: your primary residence— house, condo, cooperative—is not considered investment property unless the mortgage is paid in full.)

Stocks. Stocks represent ownership of a corporation; they are also referred to as equities. As a common stock holder, you have claim on the company's earnings and assets. Very broadly, there are several types of stocks: large cap, mid cap, and small cap; value and growth; domestic and international.

Large cap, mid cap, and small cap refer to the size of the company. If measured by the company's sales, large cap is defined as a company with sales in excess of $1 billion, and small cap is defined as a company with sales below $500 million. Mid cap, as the name implies, is in the middle. Another way of determining the size of the company is to measure its market capitalization, or multiply the stock price by the number of shares outstanding. In this instance, large cap is defined as a capitalization of $5 billion or more; mid cap is between $1 and $5 billion; small cap is less than $1 billion.

Value and growth refer to styles of investing. Value investors seek bargains, meaning the price of the stock is trading at a discount; growth investors focus on stocks with earnings growth that are above average.

Domestic and international refer to where the company is domiciled. If its headquarters are outside the United States, it is an international company—even if it has offices in the U.S.

When buying a stock or evaluating a current stock holding, take the following into consideration:

- Do you understand the company or the product/service it provides?
- Have the company's sales doubled in the last five years? (Sales are also called revenues.)
- Is the company's preferred stock noted as none or less than 10 percent of the total number of common shares outstanding? (Preferred stock is a class of stock that has preference over common stock in the payment of dividends and the liquidation of assets.)
- Is the company's current assets to liabilities ratio 2 to 1? (Current assets are assets that can be converted to cash within a year; current liabilities are debt obligations coming due within a year.)
- Is the company's debt to equity ratio 25 to 75? (The company's total liabilities divided by total shareholder equity—this shows whether the company's owners' equity can cushion creditors' claims in the event of liquidation.)

You can find this information in many places. At your local library, ask for the Value Line Investment Survey. Check online at the company's Web site (see the Annual Report), or go to the finance section of Yahoo. From Yahoo's home page, select "Finance," enter the stock's ticker symbol or select "symbol look up" to find it, and read the following sections: SEC Filings, Income Statement, and Balance Sheet.

A word about *mutual funds*, once the investment vehicle available exclusively to institutions and the well-heeled and now the investment darling for everyone. A mutual fund is a collection of stocks, bonds, or other investment vehicles owned by a large group of investors. The investors pool together their money and invest using the expertise of a professional fund manager.

There are approximately twenty thousand mutual funds available to investors, covering all areas of the market. Though too numerous to list here, the types of mutual funds in which you can invest mirror the stock market. Consequently, you can invest in stocks, bonds, or other investment vehicles via mutual funds.

Mutual funds are either no-load or load. Load funds sell shares with a sales charge. For example, if you invest $1,000 into a fund with a 5 percent load, you've actually invested $950 into the fund.

When buying a mutual fund or evaluating what you already own, take the following into consideration.

- *Turnover Rate.* This is the measure of a mutual fund's trading activity. You want a fund with a low turnover rate—the ideal target is less than 20 percent.
- *Top-Ten Holdings.* These are the individual securities held within each mutual fund. If you own or are considering more than one mutual fund, you want there to be minimum overlap in terms of the top-ten holdings of each fund.
- *Portfolio Management.* This refers to the person or team of persons responsible for selecting the securities held

by the mutual fund. Ideally, you want the manager or team of managers to have managed the fund for five or more years.

- *Expense Ratio.* This represents the percentage of a mutual fund's assets deducted each year for expenses—it's a fund's cost of doing business. All things being equal, when comparing funds to one another, select the fund with the lowest expense ratio.
- *Investment Objective.* Each fund has a primary goal (e.g., current income, capital appreciation, preservation of capital). You want a fund for which there is a consistency between its stated investment objective, its composition, and the top-ten holdings.
- *Cash Allocation.* You want a fund that is fully invested at all times; you do not want the fund to be "sitting" on cash or waiting on the sidelines before getting into (or back into) the market. Look for the cash allocation to be 20 percent or less.
- *Performance.* A special note about performance: A common disclaimer in the investment community is, "Past performance is not an indicator of future results." This is a good caveat to follow as it helps to manage your expectations and serves as a stop-gap to prevent you from chasing last year's best performer, which may turn out to be this year's dud. That said, past performance can provide insight as to a fund's performance trend and help you determine if it passes the Rule of 72 litmus test. The Rule of 72 answers the question, What return will I need to double my money within a certain amount of years? For example, if you are looking to double your money in five years, your target rate of return is 15 percent. This number is derived by using the following calculation: divide 5 (the number of years) into 72. The Rule of 72 estimate is 14.4 percent, which rounds up to 15 percent. Alternatively, you could ask how long it will take to double your money at 12 percent. The answer is six years.

Some final thoughts on assets before we shift our focus to the liabilities side of the balance sheet. Whether you are investing in bonds, income-generating real estate, stocks, or mutual funds, it is imperative to remember that you only own *your* particular investment, not the entire market! The performance of your investment and portfolio is tied to your underlying holdings. As such, it is important to:

- decide if you are going to be a trader, long-term investor, or both, and manage your portfolio accordingly
- buy and sell your securities and real estate based on guidelines, not emotions
- take into consideration how your buy and sell decisions will impact your *entire* portfolio
- look at your investments, taxable and tax-deferred (retirement based investing such as 401(k), 403(b), IRA, and so on) in aggregate—in other words, be diversified
- review your portfolio quarterly and rebalance it annually
- know the tax implications of your buy and sell decisions
- compare your investment performance to relative market indices. For example, if you hold a small cap value mutual fund, don't compare the return to the Standard & Poor's 500 Index, a large cap benchmark. It should be compared to the Russell 2000 Index

Now to the liabilities side of the balance sheet. A liability is anything that you owe; it represents an obligation to pay another in accordance with an expressed or implied agreement, and it may or may not be secured. Some liabilities qualify as "good" debt, which is debt used to finance an asset (house, college education, business venture). Other liabilities qualify as "bad" debt, which is consumer debt incurred to finance a lifestyle.

The most common line items on the liability side of your balance sheet are mortgage, car note, student loan, personal loans, and credit cards. Here are some guidelines.

Personal Mortgage. Ideally, your mortgage payment should represent 30 percent or less of your monthly income. And if the option is available with your lender, consider paying half of your monthly mortgage payment on the first of each month and the balance of it on the fifteenth—in essence a biweekly payment. Your monthly mortgage payment remains the same, but the benefit of paying your mortgage every fifteen days is that you don't pay interest on the half-payment made in the middle of the month. Thus, you end up making an extra payment over the course of the year, which adds up over the course of years! It reduces your overall interest costs and enables you to pay off your mortgage sooner.

Credit Cards. Pay the balance in full each month, or pay at least $10 more than the minimum amount due.

I am in the camp that doesn't believe debt in and of itself is bad. It all comes down to whether you are managing it versus it managing you. It is important to be strategic with the debt you incur and to formulate an exit plan *before* you get into debt. Is it too late for that? Well, commit to retiring your lifestyle debt first and to being strategic and having an exit plan for any new debt you may acquire.

The Debt Square is a useful tool for evaluating the debt you currently have and for filtering decisions about future debt.

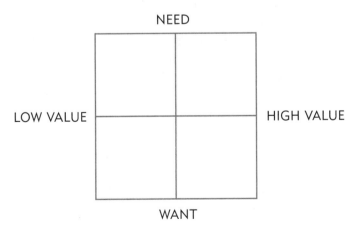

Apply the following rules to the debt you have or may consider taking on in the future.

> Low value, want—*Danger zone*
> Low value, need—*Proceed with caution*
> High value, need—*Could help you achieve your goals*
> High value, want—*Maybe, if other higher priorities are taken care of*

Completing the Debt Square, along with listing each debtor, the total amount of your outstanding debt, your monthly payments, and whether it is good or bad debt will help you get a very clear picture of your debt profile and how best to tackle any debt that is sabotaging your financial well-being.

When it comes to managing your balance sheet, you want to minimize your liabilities and maximize your assets. Having more of the former hampers your ability to have more of the latter—said another way, it hinders the degree to which your money can work *for* you.

Likewise, if the assets you own are not in line with your goals, you slow down the likelihood that you will be able to finance your goals. Let's use buying a house, a common goal, as an example. If you are looking to buy a house within five years or less, the money you are setting aside for the down payment would be invested in a cash instrument (high-interest-bearing savings account, money-market mutual fund, or certificate of deposit). You would never invest the money you are saving or already have accumulated for your down payment directly in the market via stocks or equity mutual funds. Yes, historically, the long-term performance of stocks outperforms the long-term performance of bonds, but the short-term volatility is too unpredictable to take what amounts to an unnecessary risk.

The ongoing cycle is to:

- identify your goals, with all the necessary particulars
- have, at a minimum, the amount you need to finance your goals as your savings target

- select investment vehicles in accordance with the time frame associated with your goals

If necessary, you should employ separate accounts for each goal or group of goals if that will make the overall management of your portfolio easier.

I dedicated a lot of space to Habit #6 because there is too much at stake not to. To start, your balance sheet is the true measure of your wealth just as it is for your mate. Too frequently, people make the mistake of measuring wealth by what one earns. That is too limiting in terms of providing an accurate picture of one's financial health. You can earn a lot and spend it all, or earn a lot and owe a lot as well. Earning a lot doesn't automatically mean you are financially healthy. This is extremely critical to understand, because as you evaluate your financial compatibility with your mate or your intended, you want to make certain you are in alignment on this front. And if it is the case that you aren't, then use this as an opportunity to explore how you two can come to a middle ground that works for both of you.

Likewise, and this presumes you both are coming to the table with investments of your own, the balance sheet can help you assess if you are both conservative or aggressive investors, or if your styles are opposite. If opposite, how do you make investment decisions about money that you may pool together?

Finally, when you are part of a couple, how you manage your individual and collective balance sheets will always be dictated by the fact that you have "yours, mine, and ours" goals.

Habit #7: Track Your Time

Many people experience frustration about time, wanting more of it when more cannot be created. Their problem is that they mistakenly believe they can manage time. Newsflash! You do not, I repeat, do *not* manage time! Just as you don't manage money, you certainly do not manage time. There are 60 minutes in an hour, 24 hours in a day, 168 hours in a week, 52 weeks in a year—you get the picture. Unlike money, which we can each possess in varying amounts, when it comes to time, everyone has the same amount with which to work.

But you can make choices that make you *feel* as though you are managing your time (and your money) and managing it well. Doing so, however, requires thinking differently about how you "spend" time. Ask almost anyone what they did an hour, week, or month ago, and they can easily consult their calendar and give you a rundown of their activities. Here's the more insightful question, though: could they say if that was the best use of their time *at* that time? Could you? It's a slightly different question than asking what you did last night, last week, or last month, and that difference has a profound impact on the condition of your finances.

Over the years, what I have noticed is that those who have strong balance sheets (or who are actively moving in that direction) have something in common in terms of how they manage their time. No, they don't work ad nauseam; actually, they play just as hard as they work. However, they are extremely focused, regardless of what they are doing. They don't confuse being busy with being productive, and they tend to eschew the modern-day time management principle of multitasking. They actually multitask as infrequently as possible. Imagine that!

They spend time well from the perspective that they respect the inextricable relationship between time and money, but they don't erroneously assign them equal value. They recognize that an unequal exchange is going on, and they fully appreciate that unlike money, which can be replaced, time, once used, cannot. (That is one of the reasons why they aim for more passive income—earnings from investments—than active income—earnings from the work they do.)

Likewise, they acknowledge that both time and money are "spent." And how you spend your time (and money) expresses your values and priorities. The effective use of your time is the common denominator between fulfilling your goals (Habit #5) and growing your money (Habit #6), making it critically important to know if what you are doing with the 168 hours you have each week is, in fact, the best use of your time! What is "best"? The details are extremely personal; only you can define how you should be spending your time. But a very good indicator of the connection between the "best" use of your time and how you are actually spending it is how you feel at the end of the week. Do you feel completely drained of energy, physically and emotionally? Do you dread Mondays but look forward to Fridays? Do you feel tired physically, yet energized emotionally? A yes, yes, and yes means it is time to reevaluate the choices you are making. The first two yeses are red flags; the third yes is a yellow flag, as it may simply mean you need to do a better job of pacing yourself.

How are you using your 168 hours? Literally track what you do from hour to hour, day to day, to get a true picture of your day versus what you think you are doing with your time or would like to say you are doing with it. You are bound to make some interesting discoveries! Then answer these questions.

- How have you previously viewed the relationship between your time and your money?
- What does your balance sheet reveal about your perspective?
- How will you view the time/money trade-off going forward?

Habit #8: Make Stress Your Friend

WebMD has one of the best definitions, in my opinion, of stress: "Stress is what you feel when you have to handle more than you are used to." I am sure we can all relate to this statement, personally and professionally. In fact, do you ever feel that you have more to handle than your current capacity allows when it comes to money and time? At one point, perhaps even now, have you felt that you:

- are carrying too much debt?
- have more money going out (expenses) than money coming in (income)?
- lack sufficient savings?
- lack sufficient discipline?
- juggle competing priorities?
- would have more—more money, more things, more time—if your spouse or significant other were better with money?
- were financially unprepared for a job loss, or the loss of a major client if you own a business?

By no means is this meant to be an exhaustive list of what can trigger financial stress. I ask you, though, to look beyond the specific examples and to instead focus on the universal life lessons embedded in these, and actually all, stress triggers. In doing so, you can turn stress into your friend.

Lesson #1: Pay Attention

Frequently, the thing that is causing you stress didn't happen overnight. It's been building up over time and eventually reached that point where it was more than you could handle. In other words, it tipped into stressful territory.

Action to take: Commit to paying attention to what is happening around you, to you, for you, and in you. The more tuned in you are, the less stress you'll have, because there will be fewer surprises to catch you off guard.

Lesson #2: Accept What Is

There is an insidious element to stress that has absolutely nothing to do with the trigger and everything to do with how you look at the trigger and the resulting consequences. It can be summed up in one word: acceptance. Part of the issue with stress is that it is often caused because the way things are is different from what is desired. Let's say carrying too much debt is causing you stress. The debt in and of itself isn't necessarily what is causing you discomfort; the source of the unease is the fact that even though the debt was amassed gradually, you want it to disappear right away. The "what is" is different from the "what you desire"! It is important to recognize that what is often described as stress is actually the friction created when the reality of what you are experiencing does not line up with what you had expected or wanted.

Action to take: Stay in the present moment. It may sound cliché, but it is truly the only way to mitigate the physical and emotional effects of stress. Don't longingly look back to try to rewrite the past; likewise, remember that your future is created now with the choices you make in the present moment.

Lesson #3: Remember Perfection Is an Illusion

None of us can escape the reality of having made a financial mistake or misjudgment in the past, nor is it likely that we will completely avoid doing so again. Yet you wouldn't necessarily know this given the plethora of financial to-dos, don't dos, information, and tips that abound, all of which seem to be geared toward helping you do the impossible—avoid making a mistake. And you definitely wouldn't know this based on our society's cultural proclivity to be perfect.

Actions to take:

- Look for opportunities to make stress your friend. You might as well, since stress is a natural part of life.
- Recognize that some mistakes are simply unavoidable.
- Remember that life is designed in such a way that often your most valuable lessons come through mistakes (be they your own or another person's). Besides, perfection deludes you into paying more attention to the outcome (for example, getting out of debt) rather than to the process that leads to the outcome (for example, looking at your beliefs, thoughts, and behavior with money).

- Focus less on being perfect and more on having a plan of action for when you do make a mistake. Having a workable plan is the best way to turn a mistake into a learning tool, which can become a springboard for peace.
- Keep in mind that peace comes from acknowledging your mistake and creating boundaries to ensure the same mistake doesn't occur again.

What triggers financial stress varies from person to person, as does the degree of stress felt. But the next time you feel the scales have tipped and your financial demands exceed your capacity, choose not to become overwhelmed. Look at it as life's way of signaling to you that you are ready to handle more! So instead, welcome the experience. It comes to teach you a valuable lesson that you'll only get if you pay attention, stay present, and release any attachment you may have to being perfect.

Before we press on to review the rest of the habits, think about habits one through eight. These habits individually and collectively play a role in the relationship you have with money and, thus, the condition of your finances. Yet, you may be wondering what the heck any of this has to do with the mate you have or want. It has everything to do with it!

You may have never articulated it, you may not even be consciously aware of it, but the truth is you either want someone with similar habits or someone who is the exact opposite of you. If you have habits that you consider good, then you want someone with similar tendencies. Likewise, if good habits are not your strong suit, then you want someone who is going to complement you in that regard.

Go over habits one through eight again, this time focusing less on you and more on your mate or the person you are dating. (If no one is immediately on the horizon, view these as things to look out for.)

- Are you comfortable with the manner in which he responds to stress?
- Does she seem to crumble under pressure, or does she confidently rise to the occasion to do what is necessary?
- Knowing what you know of the goals he has for himself and what you are looking to do as a couple, do you feel he is making the best use of his time?
- Do your spending policies and general approach to spending money complement one another, or are you operating at cross-purposes?

Ultimately, you are looking to discover and give voice to the ways in which you want him or her to be the same as you, as well as the ways you *need* your partner to be different in order for both you and your union to be stronger.

Habit #9: Follow the Universal Principle of Giving and Receiving

As I say in every workshop, I'm not looking to use this as a platform to espouse my spiritual beliefs about money. Having said that, I believe it would be irresponsible of me not to point out that there are both practical and mystical elements to money. This duality, much like the principle of gravity, exists regardless of your spiritual or nonspiritual beliefs.

The Quakers have a saying: "When you pray, move your feet." What I love about this proverb is that it reminds us that we have a part to play in the manifestation of our blessings, in whatever form each blessing may take. If you want any aspect of your financial story to change (be it to have more earnings, more savings, a better structured portfolio, more spending power, or less debt), *you* have to be willing to change on some level. Change what? Change any of the beliefs or thoughts you have about money, your behavior with it, or aspects of your reasoning process.

Working with money is an inside-out exercise. And one way to bring about the outcomes you desire is to give some of your income away. If your hand is closed, you not only can't give any-thing but you also can't receive anything. Similarly, if your hand is wide open, you can do both.

The practice of giving and receiving is extremely difficult to do when you are experiencing hard times. Yet that is precisely when you need to give, even if you deem what you give to be nominal. Doing so sends a message that you are operating from a space of abundance and not scarcity.

Habit #10: Know Your Credit Score

When was the last time you pulled your credit reports and checked your credit scores from TransUnion, Experian, and Equifax, the three leading credit-reporting agencies? If you are like most people, you don't pull your credit information on a regular basis, and that puts you at a disadvantage. You can pull your credit reports for free once every twelve months via www.annualcreditreport.com, and you should. (You have to pay to get your credit score.) Your creditors or potential creditors may know more about you than you know about yourself. Also, a potential employer may pull your credit report as part of their background check, and you don't want to be denied employment based on misinformation.

Pulling your credit reports on a regular basis helps you confirm that the information about you is accurate and gives you a chance to address any discrepancies. Additionally, this practice can help you identify any potential theft of identity or credit information. Likewise, if you pull your credit report before you apply for a loan or job, you give yourself an opportu-nity to improve your score, if necessary, before a loan or hiring decision is made. Please note: when you pull your own credit report, it is considered a soft inquiry, which does not negatively affect your credit score. However, if you are applying for a loan, say a mortgage or car, conduct your search for potential lend-ers within a confined, consecutive time period—for example, six straight weeks—to minimize the number of hard inquiries. Too many hard inquiries spread out over time on your credit report may scare potential lenders. They may assume, rightly or wrongly, that you are in dire financial straits.

Habit #11: Delegate, but Don't Abdicate

You may want to hire a financial advisor—whether that is a traditional broker, affiliated financial advisor/asset manager, or independent financial advisor/asset manager—to help you manage and grow your money. A financial coach can help you think about and behave differently with your money. An attorney can help you with estate planning matters or anything else requiring legal expertise (e.g., buying a home). At a minimum, I believe you should hire an accountant to help you minimize your tax liability.

Whether your financial team consists of one or several professionals, it is important to keep in mind that it is *your* money. Remember, you are outsourcing to get a level of expertise you don't have, to make the best use of your time, or to get ideas, guidance, and direction you aren't able to give to yourself. We all lack a certain degree of objectivity about our money, which a financial team can provide. However, it is imperative that you remain engaged in the process and don't abdicate the responsibility for your money to someone else. (See appendix D for suggestions on how to interview potential members of your financial team.)

Habit #12: Don't Count What You Do Not Have

Have you ever made a decision based on money you were anticipating, only to discover that the money didn't show up, or it did—but not in the amount you were expecting? Those who are most susceptible to doing this are people whose compensation is tied to bonuses, who own a business, or who work as self-employed freelancers. But other employees are prone to do this as well when they spend a raise before it arrives. The danger of counting what you don't have is self-evident, and if you have ever done it you know from firsthand experience that it can have disastrous consequences.

So do not count the funds as yours unless the client's check has cleared, the funds have been wired to your account, the client's credit card has been charged, or the bonus check or raise is in your account. This habit will force you to be conservative in both your projections and behavior where otherwise you might be foolishly aggressive.

Habit #13: Protect Yourself

It is amazing how hard people work for their tangible and intangible assets, yet they do not work as hard to protect these assets, their loved ones, or themselves in the event of injury, disaster, or death. Insurance helps protect you while you are alive. A health care proxy protects your wishes if you are alive but incapacitated or unable to express them yourself. And a will protects your wishes when you pass away. (See "General Docs" on page 91 for a detailed list of important documents that pertain to protecting yourself.)

Habit #14: Find Your Rhythm, Don't Simply Follow a Routine

This entire book is filled with a combination of what-tos, how-tos, and why-tos. But none of it will stick unless you make the process of incorporating the suggestions of this book (or any other for that matter) your own. Hence, I suggest that you find your rhythm rather than simply following a routine. Why? Routines are all about *what* you do; rhythm is about *how* you do it. Rhythm is what tailors the details of the routine to fit your style and match your preferences—it is how you make the routine your own.

For example, Habit #1 is to track your money. Some of you will use a paper-based system to do that, others will use an Excel spreadsheet, and others still will use a financial software package. As it pertains to investing, some of you will invest in stocks or mutual funds only, others of you will do a combination, and others still will add real estate to the mix. You get where I'm going. I am emphasizing a point made earlier: there isn't a singular approach or solution that will work in equal measure for everyone.

If you don't personalize a routine, it can become taxing, boring, mundane. When this happens, you run the risk of feeling stagnant, heavy, and uninterested. Then you run the risk of not doing what you know is ultimately in your best interest.

Rhythm, on the other hand, is all about flow; it is how you design the routine so it feels natural to and for you.

Habit #15: Get Some Rest

Some people are sleep deprived because they, unfortunately, suffer from a sleep disorder. More often than not, however, sleep deprivation is due to the harried lives many of us lead. Your body isn't the only thing that suffers from the lack of sleep. In general, you tend to make poorer decisions when you are tired and operating at less than full capacity. When it comes to money, the result of your fatigue is that you tend to spend haphazardly and usually on impulse.

Since you are already tracking your money (Habit #1), why not add another dimension to the exercise? Take note of how you are feeling as well. Filter the review of your spending pattern through the prism of whether you were feeling happy or sad, well rested or fatigued, when you made a purchase or financial decision. It may be hard to keep feeling tired at bay, but you can keep yourself from making poor financial decisions when you are tired. Put any purchase or decision that was clearly the result of fatigue on your "I will not do this when I'm tired" list.

Habit #16: Schedule Daily Quiet Time

I have suggested each of the previous fifteen habits with the intent of helping you get better at something with regard to your money. I don't know your particular details, but I suspect you want more of something (in addition to wanting more intimacy with your money and your mate). Is it more money, more discipline and control, more investment knowledge, more confidence, more success, or a combination of all these? In order to bring about the "more" that you want, I am going to encourage you to *slow down*!

Being busy has become a fact of modern life, and I gather that like most people you are crunched for time. Your calendar is overbooked with personal and professional commitments, and multitasking (though proven to be ineffective) has become second nature to you. But are you aware of the potential costs of your busyness? For example:

- What opportunities are you missing due to always having a hectic schedule?
- What ideas are you not fully giving birth to because you are too busy to daydream?
- What have you overlooked because you made a move before taking the time to sit down and write up a plan? Did you move from point A to point B without thinking it all the way through?
- What resources are you taking for granted or not fully utilizing?
- How might your efforts to create financial intimacy with your mate in the past have been hampered because you had just enough energy to fight it out or simply remain silent, but not enough to have a meaningful conversation?

I once worked with a business coach, Laura Berman Fortgang, who advised me to "get quiet more often and let the dream find you." Her point was that I needed to slow down and get off the "busy" treadmill if I truly wanted to discover the answers to my questions—if I wanted to discover the best way to go about achieving my goals.

I have come to wholeheartedly believe that the answers you seek are waiting on you. But you will not connect with those answers if you are in a constant state of busyness. Likewise, as more is demanded of you, the more critical it becomes for you to take time to get quiet.

How do you get quiet? I suggest setting aside ten minutes each day to do *absolutely* nothing! This is an excellent way to condition yourself to slow down and not succumb to the seduction of confusing busyness with productivity. And during your quiet time, don't talk, read, or write—just be. The cumulative effect of this practice is immeasurable.

Fair warning: the answers you seek rarely come during your quiet time, but they always come!

If you are someone who already practices silence, great! Keep it up. If not, try it for the next seven days. You might be surprised by what you discover!

Habit #17: Practice Gratitude

For all of us at any given moment, there is something that we want or want more of, yet don't have. It can be a material thing, a goal still unachieved or dream unfulfilled, a mate or a deeper connection with the one you have, or a reconciliation with a family member or friend. Often, it is easy to hone in on what is absent and hard to focus on what is present. You may not be able to or even want to say thank you *for* everything in your life or the world around you, but it is critically important to develop the practice of saying thank you *in* the midst of everything. This is much easier to do if you remember that gratitude is a state of mind; it is not tied to a particular process or outcome.

Does practicing gratitude mean that you adopt a Pollyanna viewpoint, dismissing negative experiences or disappointments? No. However, grateful people understand the connection between the practice of gratitude and the law of attraction. They embrace the notion that a grateful heart is what ultimately draws to them that which they are seeking. The saying "like attracts like" resonates with them. And grateful people tend to be more productive, compassionate, empathetic, and joyful.

Habit #18: Give Yourself Credit for What You Do Well

As you read through the aforementioned habits, I am sure there were some that are already part of your financial repertoire. Likewise, I am certain there are others on this list that you have tried and you know you'd benefit from doing but struggle with doing consistently. And then there are those that you have never even considered. Reviewing the list may remind you of what you didn't do but wished you had, or did but wished you had not.

In today's culture, it is so easy to get bogged down with self-improvement to-dos and not-to-dos (including the suggestions I've offered) that it is easy to forget to acknowledge your strengths. Personally, I believe it is just as important to know what you need to get better at as it is to know what you are proud of. To me, this is paramount if you are to operate from a space of strength that is steeped in self-knowledge, self-awareness, and self-acceptance—critical ingredients for deepening your connection and creating financial intimacy, not just with yourself but with your mate as well.

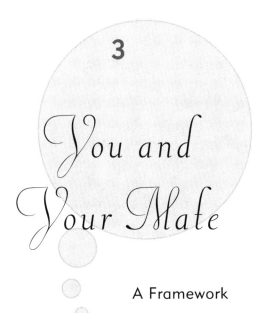

3

You and Your Mate

A Framework
for Intimacy

"How people care for each other, how they share
responsibility, power, and authority—those are
the key issues in relationships."

—SONDRA E. SOLOMON

Setting the Tone

The amalgamation of love and money has existed since time immemorial. But financial intimacy is a nascent phenomenon—the next frontier, in my opinion, for helping to bring couples closer together. Money no longer has to be the culprit for emotional and financial discord. It can now be the unlikely tool that facilitates what couples learn about each other and how they grow together.

We've already set the groundwork for getting to know what makes your story yours. Having spent time getting better acquainted with your own story, you now have what you need in order to unabashedly share it—the good and the bad—on a deeper level with your mate. At the same time, creating intimacy with yourself has prepared you for the process of getting to know the intricacies of your mate's story. This discovery and exchange are sorely needed because, if you and the two of you are like most individuals and couples, your stories have gone unexamined and untold for far too long.

And very few things in life expose your successes, setbacks, and aspirations as much as your financial story does. What you are able to hide from the world, you can't hide so easily from the person with whom you share a pillow.

Money is akin to having a third party in your relationship that showed up on the first date, never went away, and is constant and absolutely necessary. Money supports your lifestyle. It also amplifies what is working in your relationship as well as what needs to be worked on. It unmasks how comfortable you and your mate really are talking about money and the emotions you associate with it.

Intimacy takes on different forms, such as emotional, intellectual, spiritual, social, or physical. One or all of these can exist without financial intimacy, but financial intimacy cannot be experienced without any of the others. And what's tricky about intimacy, regardless of the type, is that it is nearly impossible to create with someone else if you haven't embarked on a journey of creating it within yourself.

Additionally, organic intimacy cannot be forced. It is born over time from shared moments that foster feelings of closeness, safety, and trust. In fact, you tend to measure your connection to someone through the prism of intimacy: the deeper the connection, be it with a family member, friend, work colleague, or romantic partner, the more intimate the relationship. Intimacy may be hard to define with words, but you know it viscerally. You know how it feels and when it is present because it is a special bond that is not shared with everyone.

To create financial intimacy with your beloved, you and he or she must engage in meaningful conversations that add depth to the connection you share. Doing so, however, requires that you each tap into a realm that, on the surface, has absolutely nothing to do with money, yet everything to do with it at the same time. You can't easily measure this realm because it's not about dollars and cents, but it is precisely why you and your mate have different money styles. It is the leading cause for the financial strife you will experience from time to time. It is one of the primary reasons you may each find talking about money so taxing and unpleasant. And it is exactly what will help the two of you define financial intimacy in a way that makes sense for your particular relationship.

The realm of which I speak encompasses the emotional, philosophical, and spiritual natures of money, areas that rarely get explored when it comes to money. It is far easier either to not talk about money at all or to confine the conversation just to the mechanics, which is rather ironic, when you consider that the other elements are what most shape how you show up for relationships and define what you expect from yourself and your mate when it comes to money.

The probability that you and your mate reached adult-hood with little to no formal training regarding your personal finances is quite high. More than likely, you've each made financial choices by relying on your families, friends, and society at large for guidance, direction, and feedback. Likewise, there is a natural tendency to look to your past experiences—your financial successes and blunders—for clues on what choices you should avoid or repeat in the future. All of this coalesces to mold your respective financial identities and should be examined to better appreciate what you have in common and to understand your differences.

Let's suppose you are in a relationship and you haven't yet asked any direct questions about financial history, style or preferences, values, goals, or priorities. How would you assess if you two were like-minded in the areas that are important to you, different in the areas that could be potentially dangerous, or different in the areas where the differences would actually make you as an individual and your relationship stronger? What would you look for?

Suppose you have been in your relationship for some time and it is your desire to create a "new" relationship with your mate in the area of money. How would you create it?

Habits are the behavioral manifestation of many things, including one's thoughts, beliefs, discipline, values, fears, expectations, hopes, and dreams. Since they are a combination of what you each inherited from your family and developed on your own, we are going to use habits to provide the necessary context for building your framework for financial intimacy. We have already focused on your habits; now we are going to take a look at your mate's habits.

You are going to ask your mate questions about his or her habits that may, at times, feel intrusive (for new relationships) or awkward (for existing relationships). As you work your way through this framework you will, more than likely, experience a degree of inner discomfort. It is a common and normal feeling. But knowing that you aren't asking a question of your mate that you haven't asked of yourself is a powerful way of dealing head-on with any unease that may surface. It is precisely why our approach involves converting some of the suggested habits from the last section into questions here. Likewise, you will be able to share your answers, or at least where you are in the process of formulating your answers. There are two primary benefits of this tactic: what you are able to discover about each other in the process helps you and your mate forge a stronger financial bond and deepens your emotional connection; and it is a way of illuminating what you learn from thinking through the questions.

The questions serve a multilayered purpose. You can view them as:

- a "script" of questions to be asked directly
- behaviors to observe
- ways to segue into areas of conversations that will help the two of you explicitly and implicitly connect over the practical, emotional, philosophical, and spiritual natures of money

A special note of advice to those of you who are already in a relationship, be it seriously dating, living with someone, or married: look at your mate's habits with a "new" set of eyes. Make room for fresh discoveries by letting go of what you already know or think you know. This posture will prove extremely beneficial if past money issues have in any way fractured the relationship.

And for all readers: your mate's answers are important, but not for the reasons you might suspect. Essentially, each question in this section is a closed-end question requiring a yes or no response. In some instances, the "right" answer is yes, and in others it is no. Your mate's answers certainly provide you with information about him or her, but more revealing is your reaction to the answers. What does each yes or no mean to you in relation to what you want, need, or prefer?

Additional talking points are provided as suggested follow-up questions. The details gleaned from these will give you insight as to how your mate thinks and the "why" behind his or her thinking, both of which are extremely valuable when it comes to two essential aspects of financial intimacy: compassion and understanding.

A Good Place to Start

Question #1: Do you know how much money you spent last year and on what items?

For those of you who are dating, I realize you may feel a bit squeamish about asking this question. But notice you aren't asking anything about the specific dollar amounts. The inquiry simply relates to the degree to which your mate is aware of what he has and what he tends to do with what he has.

The ideal answer is yes. But what does it mean to you if he says no and your response is yes? What about the reverse? Or what if both of your answers are no?

If you are in a relationship, what does it mean if one or both of you say no? How does a no by either or both of you impede the ability for the two of you to meet your individual goals and the goals you've established for your relationship? Keep in mind this question isn't just about typical household expenses; it also includes discretionary and disposable cash.

Question #2: Do you have a policy for how you spend your cash, use your credit card, or handle debt?

Presuming the answer is yes, what brought about the particular policy? Was it developed in response to an earlier financial mishap? Was this something she experienced or observed? Under what circumstances, if any, has she ever broken her rule? Do you have similar policies?

For existing couples, is there a spending threshold or are there parameters about what items can be bought without having to consult each other? How do you manage it if either of you breaks the rule? Does the idea of consulting with your mate before you make an expenditure cause the hair on the back of your neck to curl? Why or why not? What if you were fine with this arrangement and she wasn't? Does the notion of checking in with someone or having her check in with you feel controlling?

Question #3: Do you go to the ATM more than twice per week?

Does this seem like an odd question? Think about it: if your mate consistently goes to the ATM more than twice per week, it probably means he is underestimating what it takes to live his lifestyle or to meet his responsibilities. This is a subtle question that provides a lot of insight into how good he is at planning. The ideal answer is no.

Question #4: Do you save? Do you save before you pay your bills?

The right answer, of course, is yes to both questions, and practicing this discipline is deeply rooted in the principle of paying yourself first. Does the answer provided match with your savings philosophy and approach to managing bills? Are the two of you in sync, or are you dissimilar? If the latter, can you live with the difference? If you are already living with a difference, what would it take for the two of you to be in accord? Does that mean you need to change, or that she does? Whatever her response, is it an extension of what she learned from her family, either through observation or verbal instruction? How do your family experiences compare? If you have children, what sort of example are you setting for them? Is it the example you want to set?

Question #5: Do you own any investments?

How does he make his investment decisions? Is he a self-directed investor, or does he work with an advisor? If the latter, how did he identify the professional with whom he works?

What does he own? Again, for those of you who may feel squeamish about the nature of these questions, keep in mind you haven't asked about the value of the investments, simply the type. Does he tie his underlying investments to his goals?

What's the biggest investment mistake he's made? What investment decisions is he most proud of?

As you listen to the responses given, are any red flags coming up for you? What feelings, in general, are surfacing for you? From what you can tell, are your investment approaches and philosophies similar? Are you both conservative, both aggressive, or at opposite ends of the spectrum? What do your similarities or differences mean?

For couples, do you have a joint portfolio? If so, when was the last time the two of you sat down together to look at its composition? How have you made investment decisions in the past? Is that approach working? If yes, is it really in the best interest of your family? If you have separate portfolios, do you review them collectively to coordinate and ensure that the pool as a whole is diversified? How do you synchronize everything so that your investments can support your individual and collective goals?

Have you ever asked your mate if he has a savings account or investment portfolio or holding that you are unaware of? Do you have any secret accounts?

When you think about the interlocking circles of goals, savings, and investments, does your mate seem to have a solid strategy, or is it haphazard? How does your strategy compare? Do you both own more than you owe or owe more than you own? If the latter, what is the plan to reverse the course?

Have your mate complete the Debt Square. Ask: Do you feel overwhelmed by your debt? The ideal answer is no. If you have a stronger balance sheet than he does, does that scare you? If he has a stronger balance sheet than you, how does that make you feel?

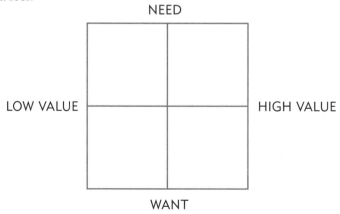

Question #6: Do you donate to charity?

Whether your mate donates to charitable organizations, gives money to strangers, or helps out family members or friends in need, speaks to her degree of generosity. Do you share a similar giving philosophy and approach? If you are a giver and she isn't, does that sit well with you? What are your feelings if you are the one who is not the giver and she is?

Question #7: Do you know your credit score?

For the squeamish among you, note that you aren't asking for the number itself—your inquiry pertains to whether or not he knows the number. Much like Question #3, this sheds light on the degree to which he is on top of the seemingly small details, details that expose a lot in terms of one's degree of financial self-awareness and financial productivity and prudence.

For those of you in a relationship, if you and your mate purchased a home or another type of property together recently, you probably know each other's score. But what about those of you who have yet to go down a path requiring you to disclose such information—do you know his score? Have you shared yours?

Question #8: Do you feel good about your finances?

There are potentially three answers your mate can provide: no, somewhat, or yes. If her answer is no or somewhat, then what would need to happen to change it to a yes? If it is yes, ask your mate what makes her most proud.

These eight questions are a great way to tap into the practical elements of money. They also happen to represent the more tangible aspects of this framework. And they are the relatively easy portion because the questions and the answers are fairly straightforward. Dig a little deeper, though, and you not only get a glimpse into the other elements that comprise your mate's relationship with money, but it prepares you for the more elusive components of that relationship as well. That is where things get really interesting.

The Jigsaw Puzzle

Numbers reveal the facts, and the facts tell a story, one that reaches far beyond what you can count. Everyone has a story, and what makes each story just as interesting as the next are the details that make a person's story uniquely complicated. Likewise, I believe people all want to tell their stories, if only they are asked—and asked in a way that allows them to be vulnerable and safe from judgment.

Hence the intentionality of the order we are following and inverting the direction from wide-to-narrow to narrow-to-wide. Think of each talking point as a different layer of information. As you move from one layer to the next, you graduate from the seemingly simple to the ostensibly more ambiguous in terms of what is discovered, revealed, and shared. One benefit of using a layered approach is that it creates a safe space for your conversations. Another benefit is that it can head off any resistance and defensiveness either of you may feel as you each travel down unfamiliar paths and retrace old paths looking for something new.

Leading with habits was preparation for the Financial Wheel exercise. Revisiting the Financial Wheel will help your mate and you get to know each other's story in a way that is totally new for both of you. Your partner should go through the Financial Wheel exercise in the same order as you, answering the same set of questions. The two of you will circle the wheel twice. The first time, your partner can connect or reconnect to what makes his financial story his.

Have your mate circle the Financial Wheel or the "picture" of the jigsaw puzzle, beginning with the *save* section. Below are the questions he needs to answer.

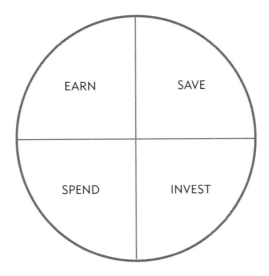

- How much do you want to save in the next thirty days?
- How much do you want to save within the next year?
- What do you want to be able to say you have saved during the course of your lifetime? Why?
- What makes the numbers you have written down important to you?
- Did you give yourself permission to think big, or did you play it safe and write numbers you felt were more realistic? If you did the latter, go back and do it again, this time letting go of any restraints that prevented you from seeing beyond what you initially thought was possible.
- How do you anticipate you will feel if you actually meet your goal at each time interval? How will you feel if you don't?

Next, have your partner move to the *invest* section. Make sure he or she understands that this section isn't about how much he or she wants to invest. Instead, you are asking your partner to consider:

- What assets do you want to own?
- Who are the people in your life that you want to be able to support?
- What causes do you want to be able to help sustain? Again, why?
- What do the assets, people, and causes mean to you?

Now you are ready for the *spend* section. As I asked you, ask your mate:

- If money weren't an issue, where would you go?
- What would you do with your time?
- What would you buy?
- What do you envision it would feel like if all this came true?
- How would you need to live your life so as to enable what you have written down to manifest?

Finally, we round out the Financial Wheel exercise with the *earn* section.

- What do you want to earn in the next thirty days?
- How much do you want to earn within the next year?
- What do you want to be able to say you've earned during the course of your lifetime?
- Why?

Ask your partner to describe the sense of achievement he anticipates he will feel upon reaching his goals. With the numbers your mate has just written, will he make his target in terms of what he intends to save? After he hits his savings target, will there be enough for him to spend it in the ways he desires?

If you are married or living with someone, I'm presuming that sharing the *earn* figures in particular isn't going to be a problem or cause any anxiety for either of you. In the case that the two of you are in the dark about each other's current level of income, this is a great way to close that information gap and explore why you haven't yet crossed that line. If you are dating and you don't feel comfortable asking for the specific number (or you don't feel comfortable sharing yours), you can do one of two things: just focus on the *why* or share a range.

If your mate's Financial Wheel is like yours and everyone else's, then he definitely has a gap between *what is* and *what he wants*. As with you, the same for him: the gap is good. It provides clues about new choices that need to be made.

Before we proceed to round two, let's spend a few moments on how you feel overall about the information your mate has shared. When you heard the *whys* behind the numbers, what did you learn that you didn't know before? Do you both err on the side of skewing your numbers toward what you believe is possible right now, or do you both give yourself permission to entertain the seemingly outrageous? Are you encouraged by her numbers because they are so close to yours, or are you scared because her numbers are so far away from yours—not even in the same ballpark? When you think about the assets your partner wants to own, the people she wants to support, or the causes she wants to help sustain, can you get on board with what she wants to do? Do you think she can get on board with what is important to you in this area?

Circling the wheel once more for round two is really for you to get a better understanding of your mate's actions, motivations, values, and perceptions. There is just one question per section of the circle, but these single questions have the potential to open a floodgate of additional queries that can facilitate ongoing conversations about all that is directly and indirectly tied to money.

- Save: How will your current savings discipline help you meet the numbers you have written?
- Invest: What needs to happen to close the gap between where you are and where you want to be?

- Spend: How could you make what you wrote down happen using the resources you already have?
- Earn: Are you fully honoring your talents, education, and knowledge with your current earnings?

Remember, in going through the Financial Wheel and asking your mate questions, you are to reciprocate and share your answers from when you did the Financial Wheel exercise. As you did round two with him or her, your mate should do the same with you.

When it comes to relationships, there are three levels of knowing. There is what you do know about each other. There is also what you *think* you know. And finally, there is what you don't know you don't know. The Financial Wheel was preparation for our next exercise, the Pyramid of Wise Money Management. It is a sequence of questions that will provide the two of you with the tools and the confidence to both deconstruct and reconstruct all three levels of knowing.

Ask your mate to tell you about the following:

- What was your first memory of money, and how has it molded your views about life, money, and the possibilities you thought you'd have?
- How has it affected the possibilities you've been able to exercise?

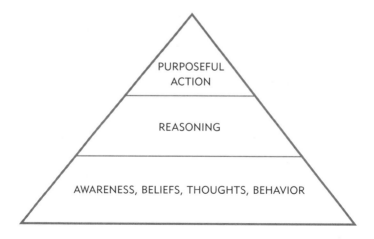

PURPOSEFUL ACTION

REASONING

AWARENESS, BELIEFS, THOUGHTS, BEHAVIOR

- Describe your family life around money. Was there lack, or was there abundance? Did you grow up thinking your family was poor, rich, or something in between?
- Do you feel you have a healthy relationship with money today? If not, what would make it healthy?
- Do you have a problem with money, either with having it (the guilt of wealth) or not having enough of it?
- What does money mean to you, and when did you first become aware of that meaning?
- Tell me how, if at all, your religious or spiritual beliefs affect how you think about money and what you do with it.
- Do popular culture and the media ever influence how you judge what you've been able to accomplish financially and the financial choices you make?
- Tell me about the first time money came up as an issue for you in the relationship we have together, if at all.
- What is important to you about money?

These questions tap into your mate's *awareness, beliefs, thoughts, and behavior* with money, the base and the foundation of the Pyramid of Wise Money Management. Remember, the Pyramid represents the pieces of the jigsaw puzzle.

Moving into the middle section of the Pyramid, reasoning, ask your mate to describe his usual decision-making process, and who, if anyone, he usually involves in the process. How does what he has described fit with what you have observed?

The base plus the middle section lead to the tip of the Pyramid—*purposeful action*. Ask your mate if he or she feels that most of the choices he or she makes are *by design* (which is ideal) or by default. For the decisions that fall into the by-default category, what needs to happen for that pattern to change?

For some of you, the aforementioned questions as well as the structure we are following are new; for others, the structure is new, but you may have already touched upon some of the questions and discussion points. If you fall into the latter category,

I want you to do two things. First, I want you to pretend you never had those earlier conversations. I don't want you to block out the possibility of learning something new. And second, I want you to compare the answers you received previously to the ones you are getting today. Are you getting more details this time around? What did you learn that you didn't know before? Since this is a two-way street, what about you? Are you sharing something for the first time, either because it never occurred to you to disclose it before or because you didn't yet feel comfortable doing so?

How your mate operates with money is a culmination of everything she does and how she thinks (which she has shared in terms of habits) and the back story that has some bearing on those habits (Financial Wheel and Pyramid of Wise Money Management exercises). Everyone operates in survive, maintain, thrive, or excel mode, or is straddling two modes. Is your mate living from paycheck to paycheck? Is he saving, but barely? Is she saving and donating money with ease? Is he able to offset expenses with passive income? Do you know this from what you are able to observe, or is it based on what has been shared with you? How does your mate's mode of operating with money match with yours? If you are not in the same mode, how does that affect your sense of financial security and your financial confidence? If you are married or living together and you are not in the same mode, how will you go about creating an agreed-upon mode for the household's finances?

What's Behind the Words

Certain words possess tremendous power mostly because their significance is derived from what you associate with them. This is especially true when it comes to money, since money evokes infinite perceptions, all of which are brought to the surface when romance is involved—sometimes overtly, sometimes covertly. Understanding what certain words mean to your mate is extremely helpful, as it will help you tap into that black hole, otherwise known as those things in the "background" quietly affecting how he feels about himself, his money, and his life.

Encourage your partner not to think too long, but to simply say what first enters his mind as you go down the list of thirteen words. As he does, write down his responses for later reflection and further discussion.

1. Trust
2. Power
3. Happiness
4. Control
5. Security
6. Dependency
7. Independence
8. Success
9. Setback
10. Preference
11. Prejudice
12. Confidence
13. Vulnerability

Did any of what he shared surprise you? If so, why? You were previously asked to think of how your mate might respond to this word association. Now that you've heard the answers, how good were you at guessing how he might respond? Have him guess at what you wrote from when you did the exercise for yourself. How good was he when it was his turn to ponder what these words mean to you? Have the two of you assumed a lot about each other in terms of your experiences with and perceptions about money and the source of both? What else have you both assumed?

Tell Me More

"Walking wounded"—that is how I refer to the human race. Each of us is who we are in this moment in time as a result of or in response to the experiences we have had. Some of the events of our lives are good, some are not-so-good, and some may be downright horrible. Whether we look at them individually or collectively, they leave an indelible imprint on our beings. How we endure and get through some of the stuff we encounter in one piece is nothing short of amazing to me at times. Yet we do.

And when we show up for *the* relationship, we bring with us the past, the present, and the future, wrapped in a package that contains our desires and a concatenation of our histories (personal, familial, and sociocultural). So when you and your mate come together, with your relationship management and communication skills in tow, which have been influenced by your experiences and refined over time but stem from your family background and upbringing, you bring to the table much that makes you each want to say, "Tell me more."

You and your mate have probably talked about past relationships, but have you ever discussed how money showed up as an issue in any of them? Do you know if your mate has traditionally been the one earning the most or the least? If she was previously married or lived with someone, do you know how she shared the responsibilities in terms of the decision-making and the expenses? Do you know if she is or is not doing things in a certain way with you as a result of what she did in a prior relationship that backfired?

You probably know if your mate grew up with his biological parents or with adoptive parents, or whether he grew up with both parents or in a single-parent household, or whether he lost a parent to an early death. But do you know anything about what he thought was missing in his household? Has he created in your relationship what he felt was missing?

You also probably know if she has (or had) siblings, and if so where she is in the birth order. But what do you know of how having siblings and whether she is the eldest, in the middle, or the youngest affects her sense of financial responsibility to her family members and to herself?

Your mate has probably described some of the ways in which money affected his childhood, but has he talked about how what he saw or didn't see affected the daydreams he had as a child, teenager, or young adult? Has he been able to turn any of those daydreams into a reality? What do you know about how his childhood experiences, in general, and with money, specifically, affect what he expects from you and the relationship you two have created? Is that expectation being met? If not, how is he expressing either his dissatisfaction or disappointment? If it is, how is he letting you know that?

Do you know what triggers your mate's anxiety about money? Do you know if you do anything to unknowingly contribute to those triggers? Have you shared your triggers?

Future historians may not look upon the years of 1960 through 2009 and see the changes that have occurred as seismic shifts to the degree we do. But right now, there is no denying that our country and world have evolved by leaps and bounds and on many levels, to boot. There were the civil rights and women's movements of the 1960s and '70s that continue through to today, expanding in definition and scope along the way. There's also the ongoing change in family structures, changing slightly with each generation. What dominated in the 1950s and early '60s—Dad as the single earner—morphed into both the husband and wife working, which morphed into an increasing number of women becoming the primary earners. Now another shift seems to be under way, back to a single-earner household, with a twist—women as the single earners. Plus, today more gay women are living openly, thereby reshaping how we define family. There's the fact that women are getting married later in life, long after they have established their own financial styles and identities. There's also our society's ever-evolving value system—the 1960s and '70s were mostly about equal pay and equal access, and the 1980s and '90s exemplified the "it's all about me at almost any cost" generation. The twenty-first century ushered in a focus on work/life balance. And then there's the fact that the current American economy is simultaneously local and global—what is local is global and what is global is local. That's a lot of change in less than fifty years!

When you talk about the politics of social change, how do history and current events influence your mate's views on money, love, work, and family? How do they affect his sense of security and stability? How does he remain grounded when so often what he cannot control is greater in scope than what he can? If your mate is a man, do any of the changes and the expectations he feels as a result affect his sense of self in terms of what it is to be a man? Did he imagine himself as Prince Charming and you as Cinderella? If so and you aren't living that out, what effect is that having on your relationship? If you are a lesbian, did your mate envision herself in a relationship where she would take on the traditional "provider" role, or was that a role you saw for yourself? If the reality you are both living out is different than what you imagined, how is each of you coming to terms with that difference?

You Know More . . . Now What?

Are you familiar with the phrase "burn the damn boat"? Its origin has been traced as far back as the ancient Greeks. Apparently, when warriors went to fight on foreign soil, they burned their boats so as to remove, literally, the option of retreating from the fight ahead of them. Returning to their boats was not an option since they no longer existed. They had to press forward and win or die trying.

Granted, you aren't fighting a war; you are creating financial intimacy. But exploring your relationship with money and how it affects the relationship you have (or hope to have) with your mate is not unlike venturing into a foreign land. This is especially true if money is akin to a foreign language for either of you. Thus, as we come to the end of this journey, I encourage you to "burn the damn boat." Here are a few suggestions as to how you can charge into this situation at full speed and embrace what lies ahead.

- Understand the difference between transactional conversations about money, which is what most people have, and the types of conversations I am promoting. Transactional conversations tend to be reactionary. What I am advocating is proactive engagement.
- Financial intimacy isn't a one-time event. Instead, it is an ongoing process that is nurtured every day in ways big and small, in ways that often have on one hand absolutely nothing to do with money, yet everything to do with what will open the door for each of you being able to be transparent, open, and honest about things concerning money.
- See beyond the obvious and know that any disagreements you may have about money have very little to do with money directly. In the same vein, commit to being engaged with your money and using it as a tool for deepening your mutual trust and respect.
- Continue to give yourself permission to question what you know to be true as well as what you presume to be true about yourself and your mate.
- Be willing to let go of some of your long-held beliefs, thoughts, and behaviors. It may be the only way you will be able to *see* what you previously didn't notice.
- Create rituals for checking in so that unpleasant surprises are kept to a minimum. Rituals are the best risk-management tool from both a financial and emotional standpoint. (The 90-Day Letter exercise in the appendix is a great tool to add to your ritual.)

- And finally, in the words of my dear friend Deno, "Don't leave your logic at home." And don't leave your grace and compassion there either. All of it is necessary when dealing with love and money.

With all that we have covered, we have touched upon the practical, emotional, philosophical, and spiritual natures of money. This is just the beginning; the more you *practice* financial intimacy, the more you will continue to learn about yourself and your mate and the more you will continue to grow together. The goal throughout has been to take you and your mate deeper into a framework until you reach the core. What's the core? The point at which you are able to define what financial intimacy feels like, looks like, and *is* for the two of you.

4

Final Thoughts

"No great thing is created suddenly."

—EPICTETUS (A.D. 200)

On Monday, September 15, 2008, Lehman Brothers, a venerable investment banking firm founded in 1850, filed for Chapter 11 bankruptcy protection; Merrill Lynch, a major brokerage firm, agreed to sell itself to Bank of America; and American International Group (AIG), one of the world's premier insurance companies, revealed it was having liquidity problems and was fighting to avoid imminent bankruptcy. Lehman Brothers' news was unfortunate, yet somewhat expected; but the news about Merrill Lynch and AIG caught all but a few people by surprise. This date will go down in the financial annals as a day the United States experienced a financial meltdown of epic proportion.

On January 2, 2008, the Dow Jones Industrial Average, an index of thirty "flagship" stocks, closed at 13,338.23 points. On September 15, it closed at 10,917.51 points. On December 31, it closed at 8,776.29. On March 9, 2009, it closed at 6,547.05, a long way—in the wrong direction—from its historic high of more than 14,000 points reached on October 9, 2007. In the days, weeks, and months following September 15, the end-of-day closings have been trending downward overall, but the day-to-day closings have gyrated wildly. One day it closes down more than 700 points; the following day it recoups some of its losses with a gain of 500 points or more. The intra-day swings are just as drastic as the end-of-day closings, and both continue. In these massive negative and positive swings there lurks the nasty monster called "volatility," not a friend of those who require stability to make decisions regarding investment and economic growth.

Right now, the economy is in a tailspin as the government attempts to get its hands around this out-of-control bear. Thus far, the measures that have been taken to return a sense of calm to the market have been ineffective and inconsistent. (Hmm, could it be because they are not getting at the root of the problem?) From my perspective, it has reached a point where it is difficult to determine what is really contributing to the market's volatility—how much of it is based on poor business and economic fundamentals across the board, and how much on unbridled panic and a general drain of investment-intended cash from the market. There isn't a perfect solution to our economic challenge, and it will take several years before we know if the measures that have been taken were the right ones. In the meantime, the deleveraging—the unwinding of debt—and the tightening of credit continues, and none of us are able to escape the effects.

In the minds of some, the seeds for this current financial crisis were planted almost thirty years ago when the federal government deregulated the lending industry. The original intent of a subprime mortgage was to act as a short-term bridge loan to cover the gap between when a buyer purchased a new property and when that same buyer sold property in another transaction but had yet to receive the proceeds from that sale. Once received, the proceeds were to be used immediately to satisfy the subprime or bridge loan.

The current fiasco—which started with the obscure repackaging of subprime mortgages before becoming a credit crisis and subsequently a liquidity crisis and finally a crisis of confidence—is due to a combination of undisciplined lending and undisciplined borrowing practices, greed, and unbridled optimism, a component of the American Dream. These factors have created an amalgamation that has turned our global financial system upside down. It has, unfortunately, prompted some to unwisely sell assets and seek safety in cash. As I can attest to from the crash of 1987, those who resisted the temptation to *feel* better and stayed in the market (as hard as it was to do) fared much, much better than those who locked in their losses by selling their assets more out of emotion than necessity.

It is the use of subprime mortgages during the last fifteen years or so that has turned a facet of the American Dream—creating wealth through home ownership—into an American nightmare. Sadly, this nightmare isn't just confined to the negligent subprime borrowers who took on much more leverage, or debt, than they should have, or the irresponsible lenders who knowingly lent money to financially vulnerable borrowers. It has also affected subprime borrowers who were acting as responsible citizens but were ill-advised and uneducated about what they were obligating themselves to. Additionally, people who are in traditional prime mortgages or those who don't even own a home are feeling the effects as well.

Current events have culminated to form what in some circles is being described as a financial volcano, and while manmade, it behaved in very much the same way as a natural one. Before a volcano erupts, there are always signs of unrest, such as trembling and vibrations. Some eruptions are quiet, while others are explosive, and some eruptions can be accompanied by other natural hazards. In a similar fashion, there were plenty of forewarnings before our financial volcano erupted; it was definitely explosive, and it triggered a global financial crisis. And like real volcanoes that cause great damage over prolonged periods in terms of loss of life and property, our manmade one is bringing about the loss of jobs, businesses, homes, and the ability to be productive. For some people fortunate enough to escape these real losses, they are frozen in place, fearful of the possibility that their foundation may crumble. It's a valid concern, since the market values of most peoples' homes and investment portfolios are down considerably. The result: a loss of confidence and faith in our economic system, which seems to worsen every day.

The financial turmoil we are experiencing might prove to be unprecedented. Not because we haven't had down markets before, but because of the factors contributing to this crisis and the fact that it has crossed the Atlantic and Pacific Oceans indiscriminately. It is affecting the markets in Western Europe and Asia to a greater degree than previous market corrections. And the fact that these regions had their own credit issues in the closet makes this financial crisis arguably more reciprocal across borders. Almost everyone everywhere is feeling the effects of this turmoil in some way, whether it is financially, psychologically, or both.

Depending upon how deeply your circumstances are affected by the current economic environment, it might be hard to see beyond this moment and do what I am about to ask you to do: try to look at the economic shift underfoot as a natural purging. Nature purges all the time. As a result of this purging, what adjustments will we make to our economic systems and policies—individually and collectively—that we never would have considered were it not for this crisis and if our comfort zones and sense of financial security had not been thrown into upheaval? Where had we become financially complacent? Good times rarely prompt questions of this sort. As such, times of prosperity can mask where you, your mate, or the both of you may be financially vulnerable.

A weak economy, on the other hand, exposes or exacerbates these areas of financial vulnerability. This makes tough economic times, ironically, the perfect time to nurture financial intimacy. It also represents the point at which financial intimacy can mean the difference between a relationship that makes it through the storm and one that becomes a casualty of the crisis. Tough times necessitate a degree of candor and transparency that can be either casually addressed or easily avoided when times are good. So if you allow it, periods of financial turmoil can actually be the times when you and your mate make tremendous strides as you continually work to reach your core. This is one of the many ironies of life: it often presents opportunities to learn and grow when you least want but most need it.

Current events also serve as a reminder that what you have worked hard to create can be undone seemingly in an instant. There are those whose lifestyles will be interrupted drastically if they are downsized as a result of the economy's woes and are not financially prepared to be out of work for an indeterminate amount of time. Similarly, there are those who have watched the market value of their portfolios depreciate considerably. This is really a tough pill to swallow, especially if the goal was to use some or all of the funds within the next five years. Herein is another lesson to take away, and ironically, it directly ties into what brought about this mess in the first place. The fundamentals are universal; what applies to governments applies to businesses and also to individuals. I call it the two Ls and a D: leverage, liquidity, and denial.

Just as it is important for you to have a healthy balance sheet, the same holds true for governments and businesses. No one, be it a person or an entity, is exempt from the fact that if a *leverage* problem emerges, it is because you have a *liquidity* problem. If you owe more than you own and are short on the necessary cash to meet your debt obligations when your creditors come calling, then trouble is right around the corner. And if you refuse to acknowledge a challenge is on the horizon or deny the full extent of the problem, you minimize your chances of making smart, strategic decisions and, if necessary, negotiating from a place of strength.

Dealing with this financial crisis has been made worse by the media's coverage of these nerve-wracking days, weeks, and months. In booms and busts, the media seems to capture the imagination and participation of many across the social spectrum—in the dot-com boom, every person capable of having an opinion had one and tracked his or her favorite pet stock with diligence. Similarly, today people who previously had no concept of what a collateralized debt obligation was have taken it upon themselves to "understand" these issues through the financial media. The media message, however, that has raised my ire is the oft-repeated "Wall Street versus Main Street." Though this comparison makes for great water cooler chat and sound bites for media, political, and even some Wall Street pundits, it is hogwash. There's just one street, Our Street. We are all in this together, whether we realize it or not and whether we like it or not, sharing the upside and the downside, and we do each other a disservice when we pit one group against the other. My personal feelings aside, there is an even greater loss when we engage in this Wall Street versus Main Street contest regarding the causes of this situation and, more important, the potential solutions.

First, we run the risk of missing the parallels between what has transpired on a macro level with the economy and what is happening on a micro level with our own financial affairs. Second, we run the risk of overlooking the fact that this financial meltdown is chock-full of lessons and important reminders.

Take for example the issue of control. Crises tend to make us feel like we have less control over things that we *can* actually control. And I understand how comforting it is to look outside for both guidance and answers, as well as to assess blame and express frustration and anger. However, too much time talking about and thinking about what you cannot control—or what others outside are doing or didn't do—is more stressful than fruitful. Plus, the feeling feeds on itself, growing to a point where you can become overwhelmed. Feeling grounded becomes vital during any crisis, but especially a financial one. And the best way to accomplish that is by focusing on *you* and the choices *you* make and the risks *you* take. Whether you are making fully or partially informed choices, your choices will always serve as your locus point.

Keeping this in mind reminds you that what you can control you should, and what you cannot control you should simply be aware of. You cannot control the decisions other people make, nor can you control the risks they take. Yet you *are* responsible for how you let the choices they make and the risks they take *affect* you. I bring all of this to your attention not because I think you lack an awareness of what you can and cannot control. Rather, it is intended to offer a prescription on how to offset what naturally happens during times of uncertainty—an inclination to pay more attention to those aspects outside the realm of your control than to what lies within your realm. And with respect to the things we can control there are certain best practices that are required of us in tough times to even consider reaching financial intimacy. These are central to the theme of financial intimacy, especially when you find yourself also having to manage the intention of one person against the perception of another.

At the moment, individuals, corporations, and our government are mired in finger-pointing, trying to lay the blame on a single "wrong" decision. What makes this a futile use of time and energy is that the outcome of anything (good or bad) is usually a by-product of a series of choices, which is why following a disciplined decision-making process is so critical. Granted, doing so won't always guarantee that you will get what you want, because you can make the right choice yet end up with the wrong result, or you can make the wrong choice but end up with right result. But a process typically minimizes the potential for unpleasant surprises. Likewise, knowing what the worst outcome could be and doing everything to avert it is wise and practical; it is not, as some believe, a demonstration of a lack of faith or negative thinking or an act of expecting and preparing for the worst. The goal is to have a strong foundation regardless of what is happening in the economy. You want the negative aspects of the market's fluctuations to affect you as little as possible. This necessitates a filtering process for making decisions, which our previous chapters have helped you formulate.

Economic downturns remind us that we cannot microwave or instant-mix a sustainable, long-lasting solution for the areas where we are financially vulnerable. Getting to the root cause of the vulnerability requires time, effort, and patience. This is really evident when it comes to leverage. When times are tough, the debt load that once seemed manageable can suddenly become an unbearable burden, and an emotion kicks in that says, "I want to get out of this *now!*" This sentiment is primarily expressed as it pertains to lifestyle debt rather than life-purpose debt. For most people, however, it always takes longer to get out of debt than the time it took to acquire the debt in the first place, unless you have an unexpected windfall. Such a fact can prove to be extremely frustrating given the instantaneous society in which we live. Immediate access to almost anything or anyone can lull you into wanting, if not expecting, a quick fix when there simply isn't one.

Another area of financial vulnerability is insufficient savings. What is the current financial environment revealing about your savings habits? And since your investments are a derivative of what you have saved, what is the current situation revealing about your investment oversight practices, another area of financial vulnerability? If you need access to a portion or all of your investment funds within the next five years, are you executing a plan to dollar-cost-average out of the market until you have in cash the amount of money your goals require? Most people are familiar with the practice of dollar-cost-averaging, or investing a fixed dollar amount at regular intervals, for getting into the market. But it is also a wise approach for gradually pulling money out of the market as well.

Are you glued to the television, constantly refreshing your Web browser, tuned into your radio, and reading your local newspaper more feverishly than ever, trying to consume as much information as you can about this global financial crisis to learn what to do, as well as what not to do? If yes, then there is no doubt that you have been greeted with a healthy dose of doom and gloom and "the sky is falling" hysteria, which only magnifies your fears—especially if you are in dire straits.

It is not my intention to minimize your concerns, fears, or the actual challenges you may have in meeting your mortgage or rent payments, paying your credit card or utilities bills, putting gas in your car, or putting food on the table. But I submit this for your consideration: there is a brighter side to all of this. Seeing it, though, requires adopting a bit of a contrarian attitude. It requires filtering out the noise of the media, at least long enough to see the blessings in the midst of this burden. And it requires actually sweating the small stuff. And maybe most of all, it requires being comfortably on the same page as your partner with respect to these matters.

In the section on habits, the very first one I presented was "Track Your Money." Some of you will embrace this habit immediately and effortlessly; others of you will reject it outright. The balance of you will make an attempt to track your money, but will stop doing it before it can really take hold and become like second nature to you. Of the things you can do with money (earn, save, invest, and spend), how you spend your money is the area in which you have the most control during challenging financial times. Sweating the small stuff involves examining your expenses to identify where your money is going and ways to scale back the amount that is going out. You want to examine both your necessary expenses as well as the discretionary ones. Sweating the small stuff involves being more engaged with your investment portfolio, but not for the purposes of making any drastic changes to your allocation or selling any of your holdings prematurely. Instead, reconnect with why you have the portfolio structure you have and potentially confirm that it remains the right way to go given the goals you have and the timing of those goals. Sweating the small stuff means letting the lessons learned from this economic downturn prepare you for the next one. All the hints you need lie with your ability to answer this question: are you meeting this downturn in a favorable position, a precarious one, or somewhere in the middle? If (or when) you are a couple, sweating the small stuff means recognizing it is easier for you and your mate to work together than for you two to be working separately and operating at cross-purposes. Sweating the small stuff means doing everything you can to take care of the job (or the clients) you have currently because getting a new job (or new clients) may take longer than it has in times past.

Times like these are perfect for reevaluating all of your habits, not just the habits of tracking your money, diligently saving, and strategically investing. Times like these remind you to pay attention to the forewarnings (they are always there) and not to wait until the situation reaches a boiling point before you begin to prepare and respond. Times like these teach the lesson that the consequences of a lack of discipline are typically more painful than the nuisance of doing what needs to be done even when you don't feel like doing it. Times like these are perfect for revealing the blind spots you may otherwise discount. Times like these are perfect for remembering how valuable it is to have financial intimacy with yourself. Times like these make you realize how valuable it is to have substantial and significant conversations about all the elements of money with your mate. Times like these perfectly reinforce the message that money can actually be one of the most romantic topics for you and your partner to discuss. Times like these allow you and your mate to discover that the differences between you in terms of your financial beliefs, thoughts, styles, and behavior don't have to mean indefinite financial incompatibility or financial doom. Instead, look at it as a call to action for the two of you to think creatively about how you can make your differences work for you. Times like these remind you to keep the long-term picture in focus, despite how distorted your view of that picture may be due to short-term activity. (A method I recommend to coaching clients is to create a vision board filled with pictures and words that represent your goals and aspirations; you want to have it located in a place you can glance at frequently.)

What am I suggesting with this brief overview of the current economic crisis and the lessons and reminders it offers you? Turn this and all challenging times into a time of opportunity by shifting how you view what's going on financially, globally, domestically, locally, and in your home, by shifting how you talk about the crisis and what you focus on, and by shifting how you handle it. Whatever you intuitively started to do in response to this economic crisis, either directly or indirectly, may hold some valuable clues for you to examine.

Eventually, our economy will rebound, and we will experience another bull market. And guess what? Some of you will forget the lessons learned during this bear market, which is extremely unfortunate since we seem to undergo a financial correction (sometimes called a crisis when it is widespread and prolonged) every ten years or so. That means we'll be back here (in a bear market) again, due to a different set of circumstances, of course. The details that bring about each bear market vary, but there is a common thread: they are usually precipitated by undisciplined decision-making methods, the inability to forecast and prepare for the worst, and greed.

So, if it is the case that you *read* this book but didn't *do* it, remember September 15, 2008, and the effects of that day's events. If it is the case that you did the work this book asks of you, don't become complacent; you need to remember September 15, 2008, and its effects as well. And if you are reading this at a time when September 15, 2008, and its effects seem like a distant memory, remember the wise words of the fictional character, Forrest Gump, from the movie of the same name: "Stupid is as stupid does."

Weathering the storms that financial crises bring about makes financial intimacy paramount, regardless of whether the crisis is the result of your own choices or the choices of others. I get chills when I think of the employees who will go home on Friday evening and return to work on Monday morning to the news that their jobs no longer exist or that they are on the brink of being terminated. (Am I describing you or your mate?) Even if your financial house is in order, news of a layoff will likely bring about a period of adjustment. And if financial intimacy is absent for the people who find themselves living out this scenario, that could potentially spell emotional and financial disaster that lingers long past the conclusion of the financial crisis.

Additional Best Practices
by Marital Status

*A*s you have probably gathered from all that you have read thus far, I believe working with money is a skill to be learned, continually developed, and practiced. In that spirit, I want to provide additional best practices that are specific to your partnership status. The following suggestions are segmented to take into account specific concerns of which I think singles, stay-at-home spouses/mates, unmarried couples living together, those thinking about separation or divorce, or those considering another marriage should be aware.

Single

Single women have special concerns that are similar to their peers who are the sole or major breadwinners in their families: you don't have a second income to fall back on. *Everything* is your responsibility. As such there are extra precautions you have to take when it comes to managing the components of your Financial Wheel, in general, and then as it pertains to dating.

Starting with your first date, the person you are dating is giving you clues about their financial character, style, preferences, identity, and habits. Don't miss the signs! Remember, the goal is to look without being judgmental. Also, keep in mind that you are seeking to learn what his consciousness around money is—not simply what his financial situation is, which is fungible. Look at his behavior.

- When he is the one planning the dates, what types of venues are chosen? Are they on the low, medium, or

high end? Do the venues seem to correspond with the assumptions you have made about his current earnings?
- Do you notice whether he pays using cash, a debit card, or a credit card?
- If he traditionally picks up the tab, at what point, if at all, do you offer to reciprocate, and how does he respond?

It is also important to look beyond the things you can see and tune into the invisible, i.e., what and how you are feeling. We may all have a bit of Cinderella in us.

- Are his behavior, in general, and his behavior with money, in particular, feeding your Cinderella complex or challenging it?
- Have any red flags been raised? If so, are you acknowledging them?
- Has anything he has done (or not done) tapped into any of your fears? For example, does he consistently order the most expensive bottle of wine on the menu? What do you notice of his tipping habits—is he generous or stingy? If you travel together, does he tend to suggest taking a connecting flight with an extended layover rather than a direct flight simply to save $50?

If you have answered yes, it doesn't necessarily mean you should run for the hills, but it does mean you may need to observe more, listen more, and ask more questions. You are looking for consistency and patterns in his behavior.

I have suggested making copies of the contents of your wallet and listed a number of important financial documents you should have stored in a safe-deposit box. If you are single and not dating anyone seriously, please make certain someone (a relative or best friend) knows how to access your safe-deposit box (or similar safe place) in the event of an emergency. If you are dating someone seriously and in a trustworthy way but not living together, make sure your partner knows how to access these important documents. And if your status should change and you are no longer single, make sure to update the stored documents accordingly. Likewise, if your status should change and you own a business, don't forget to update your business's succession plan and your estate planning documents—especially if you have a business partner.

Disability insurance is critical for single women, especially single women with children. You want to make sure you have sufficient coverage. Coverage through your employer may not be enough; it might be necessary to obtain supplemental coverage. The amount should be enough to cover your expenses, including any estimated but uncovered medical expenses, while you are recuperating—or, God forbid, the rest of your life should you become permanently disabled. Single mothers, in particular, also need to ensure they have adequate life insurance coverage.

Couples with a Stay-at-Home Mate

Regardless of how you are coupled—married or living together, male and female, or female and female—noted below are some of the things you and your mate need to address to ensure the financial security of the stay-at-home mate.

Make sure you and your mate are allocating resources for and paying into Social Security for the one who is at home. Similarly, make sure a line item is included in your budget for contributions to a spousal IRA; it is important that the one staying home has a retirement vehicle and investments in her name as well. Check with your accountant or with the Internal Revenue Service for the latest in specific rules and guidelines for spousal IRAs. Additionally, make sure the working spouse is contributing enough for both of you in his or her employer-sponsored 401(k) or 403(b) plan.

Get life and disability insurance for the stay-at-home spouse as well. (Please note: disability insurance for the stay-at-home spouse may not be available in all states.)

You and your mate will also need to decide how best to handle assets in terms of whose name the assets should be held in, such as the deed to the house or the investment portfolios. Should the assets be held in both of your names or just one? If the latter, whose? Or should the two of you create a trust and have the assets held in a trust? This is especially important if the working spouse's profession leaves her open to potential litigation. Working with an accountant and an estate planning attorney will help the two of you determine which route is best for you. Please note that dual-income households must concern themselves with this matter as well, but it seems to get overlooked more frequently when a spouse stays at home.

Additionally, it is vital for the stay-at-home partner to be engaged with the investment management aspects of your family's portfolio, even if it is a task she dislikes. Having an aversion to this component of managing money is not an excuse for being uninformed.

Unmarried Couples Living Together

For those of you living together but unmarried, it might be wise to put your financial arrangement in writing in the form of a domestic partner agreement. (You will need to check with your attorney to confirm if this agreement is valid and binding in the state in which you live.) This agreement addresses how the two of you will share income, expenses, and property, and it can provide support to other legal documents the two of you might have, such as a will.

Same-sex couples living in states that do not acknowledge civil unions or same-sex marriages may wish to have an attorney include any special concerns or considerations you and your mate may have in your domestic partner agreement. If there are children birthed during your union, the nonbirth mother should adopt the children so that you both have equal parenting rights.

For any couple with children from other relationships, it is helpful to ensure your domestic partnership agreement includes details about the financial obligations you respectively have (or do not have) for those other children.

Thinking about Separation or Divorce

They say you learn more about a person during the period that you are breaking up with him than you did during the relationship. Divorce is rough on many different levels, but your ability to navigate through the financial aspects of such an event will enhance your ability to come out on the other end with the financial freedom required to move on. You should always consult a matrimonial attorney for specific advice related to your situation and the state in which you and your partner currently reside or last resided together. That said, here is a punch list of what to either start thinking about or begin doing once you have made the decision to separate, but *before* you announce your decision to your mate! It is at this point that financial intimacy becomes more of an internal practice rather than a shared experience.

1. Make copies of:
    - the statements for any accounts held jointly—banking, investment, and debt;
    - your latest tax return;
    - your respective retirement account statements, e.g., IRAs, 401(k), or 403(b); and
    - all legal documents, such as the deed to your house or lease agreement if renting, wills, pre- or postnuptial agreements, insurance policies, and the like.
2. Run a copy of your credit report.
3. If you don't already have a separate checking and savings account, open them in your name, even if you only deposit the minimums required.
4. If you are the stay-at-home spouse, prepare a personal business plan for how you will generate income once you are no longer married.

5. If you have not been engaged with the management of the household finances, be it the day-to-day expenses or the long-term planning in terms of investment selections, begin to have a more active role so that you know what is going on.

Considering Another Marriage

Know that when you remarry, you lose your entitlement to the Social Security and pension benefits of your ex-spouse. Likewise, alimony support is usually suspended if you remarry.

You may want to prepare a pre-nuptial agreement with your new mate, especially if there are children (from either side) involved. You and your new mate may have a desire to protect the inheritance of the children from your previous marriage or relationships. If you, your new mate, or both of you have college-bound children, keep that in mind in the event your children plan to apply for financial aid.

In the End

The questions and the things to take into consideration seem never-ending, don't they? They also seem ever-changing.

We learn by asking questions first of ourselves and then of others, challenging what we know or presume we know, expanding our boundaries to include new discoveries, and allowing ourselves to shift from one way of thinking to another. However, we tend not to like the process we have to go through to acquire knowledge and wisdom; we seem to forget that in order to walk to something we have to first walk through something.

"Life is hard." These are the first three words in M. Scott Peck's seminal book *The Road Less Traveled*. I am almost certain you have experienced enough of life's ups and downs to agree with this sentiment. But why is life hard, exactly? Is it because to some degree we all have bought into a notion that says there is something out there that will one day make it all easier? Is it because you, like many others, are juggling so many balls? Is it because accepting a ball dropping is hard to do when you are bombarded with messages that view dropping a ball as a sign of imperfection? Is it because picking up the fallen ball often requires more strength than you think you have? Is it because times of uncertainty remind you that you pay a price when you don't do the work that is yours to do? Or is it because we approach things in a reactive way as opposed to being ready for them and embracing them in our consciousness before they appear as a crisis?

I don't know why life is hard for you; the reasons vary for different people. But one thing that is universal is that *living your life takes a lot of work*. No one gets a free pass on this one. Designing the life you want takes even more work! The extra work is entirely optional, though. Consciously designing your life means being willing to ask obscure questions, to imagine the impossible and think that it can actually come true, and to step into the unknown to bring about what you have envisioned. Financial intimacy falls into this zone. Hence the reason the work financial intimacy demands of you can be and feel daunting. It is a journey you have to be fully present for and participate in, in order to reap the emotional benefits and the financial ones too.

Imagine coming home and finding a large green elephant in your living room. You see it, your mate sees it, and you both acknowledge its presence. But neither you nor your mate goes a step further to question how it got in the living room or why it is there or why the elephant is green! Sounds absurd, doesn't it? Yet, in reality, this is something we do quite frequently. Often the obvious doesn't get addressed. When you ignore the obvious, you usually also miss what isn't so obvious but what is perhaps more necessary to discuss. It is similar to the illusion created by a galanty show; what is going on behind the screen doesn't always match what you see on the other side of the screen. The shadow images conveyed on the screen are not reflective of the true nature or proportions of their source. Financial intimacy works in much the same way; your degree of self-awareness, beliefs and thoughts about, and behavior with money are all projected onto the screen of your life. And peeking behind the screen is how you will discover the personal and private details of the story that is yours, your mate's, and both of yours together.

In the end, this book has been about those three stories; it has been about the intended and unintended consequences, emotionally and financially, of three converging relationships. Now you have a better understanding of your relationship with money; your mate has a better understanding of his or her relationship with money; and, combined, you each have a better understanding of where your respective stories connect to create the inevitable overlap of money and love, which can be nothing short of convoluted and messy at times. Yet chaos often precedes beauty and order. As you continue to step into the unfamiliar, mysterious, and sometimes confounding realm of financial intimacy, let it pull you closer to your core.

Acknowledgments

The work that is ours to do is never done alone, and my list of thank-yous is longer than these pages allow. Many people have cradled me throughout my life and career, but there are some who were extremely instrumental as this book evolved from an idea into the manifestation you now hold in your hands. They provided love, encouragement, guidance, feedback, and—toward the end when my work and writing schedule were absolutely insane—much needed comic relief. All of it worked together to pull me across the finish line.

My mother: thank you for signing me up for a book-of-the-month club when I was three! I truly believe my insatiable curiosity, love of words, and gift of insight stem from my early exposure to books. I also thank you for passing along an important gene: tenacity. Writing a book requires a great deal of doggedness.

My amazing group of friends, who all are way cool: Anjeanette Allen, Siddiq Bello, Sharon Bowen and Larry Morse, Evolyn Brooks, Loretta Lynch Hargrove and Stephen Hargrove, Linda Holden-Bryant, Suleman Khan (my Tea Lounge angel), Dana Michel, Marcie Moss, Sharon Pendana, Delissa Reynolds-Lyssy, Deirdre Scott, Anthony Watts and Dominic Lepere, Dorian Webb, Angela Wiggins, and Todd Wilson. Carlton Brown, Monica Meehan McNamara, and Miriam Tager, you three were a constant voice of reasoning when I needed it most, thank you! Toni Booker and Michelle Coffey, thank you for being my second set of eyes from the beginning to the end! I also want to thank Bob Hoffman and Obie McKenzie for being the soothsayers they are; I finally listened.

Laura Berman Fortgang, Mark Monchek, and Agnes Mura: the three life and business coaches with whom I have worked over the years. Thank you for helping me step more firmly into my purpose.

I am grateful for a hot, humid July evening in 2005 and, because of tired feet and too many bags, my serendipitous encounter with Colin Harrison on the B train. You introduced me to my literary agency, Dystel & Goderich, and Jane Dystel and Adina Kahn. Their representation led to the publishing house Chicago Review Press, which has, indeed, been a perfect fit for me. Thank you, Colin; thank you, Jane and Adina; and, thank you, Sue Bradanini Betz, Mary Kravenas, Michelle Schoob, Laura Di Giovine, and everyone else at CRP who believed in me and my message.

I am eternally grateful to the Honorable Johnny Baynes: thank you for the lifeline.

My other lifeline has been my AIG family, especially Rich Pluschau, Gary Muoio, Joe Costantino, JoDeen Urban, Fritz Barjon, Warren Berey, Neel Shah, J.P. Ham, and Joseph Minetti.

Diane Ricketts kept the administrative aspects of my life in order—what a blessing!

A heartfelt thank-you goes out to all my clients (past and present), workshop attendees, and subscribers to Financial Profundities. I truly appreciate the gift of your trust; thank you for your stories and your questions and for keeping me on my toes!

And there is nothing better than when a client turns into your staunchest advocate. That accolade goes to everyone at the Woodhull Institute for Ethical Leadership, especially the colleagues I now count as dear friends. I am grateful to Naomi

Wolf, Wende Jager-Hyman, Tara Bracco, Karla Jackson-Brewer, and Deborah Siegel, Ph.D. There aren't enough words.

There also aren't enough words of appreciation for the nineteen women who allowed me to interview them, some of whom are identified by a pseudonym: Glenise, Sabrina, Patrice, Delissa, Elizabeth, Leah, Christine, Shari, Mary Anne, Sasha, Miriam, Robin, Kim, Molly, Liz, Jody, Sarah, Kirsten, and Toni. Many thanks for your faith and your trust. You opened up about matters that are both personal and private and gave me carte blanche to use your experiences to tell a larger, universal story. I could not have asked for better material with which to work. You enriched my life tremendously, and I know you will do the same for everyone who reads about you.

Patti Unger did an incredible job transcribing my interviews. Thank you for making my life easier!

James Borberly, my direct contact at the Bureau of Labor Statistics: you were always available, and no inquiry was too trivial. I appreciate your help both in gathering data and interpreting the numbers.

I also want to thank two people whom I have never met but whose writings greatly influenced my approach to this book: Po Bronson (*What Should I Do with My Life?*) and James B. Stewart (*Follow the Story*).

And last but not least, the amazing staff at the Tea Lounge, my writing refuge. For seven straight months you were my home away from home, and you took superb care of me!

Finally, I thank God for showing me that I always have more than enough light to walk in and for giving me a spiritual family to walk with.

Appendixes

Appendix A

90-Day Letter

orking with money is not static, and neither is financial intimacy. It is both a practice and a process because you have to monitor your habits, reinforcing the good ones and giving up the bad. As a reiterative process, you are continuously given a chance to get feedback about the systems, policies, and strategies that are effective and the ones you need to refine.

The 90-Day Letter is an excellent tool for giving yourself feedback. It is a perfect way of ensuring that you stay on track as you incorporate your newfound financial self-awareness and fiscal fitness skills into your life on a *daily* basis.

When writing your letter, think about what you've discovered while reading and completing *Financial Intimacy*. What do you want to change? What will you have to do, be, or have in order for those changes to materialize? Both you and your mate should complete the 90-Day Letter.

Ninety days from today, (_____),

my relationship with my money and my mate will be

different than they are today because . . .

_____

_____

_____

_____

_____

_____

_____

_____

_____

_____

_____

_____

_____

_____

_____

_____

_____

_____

_____

_____

Signed by: _____

Date: _____

After completing the letter, seal it in an envelope and make a commitment not to open it until ninety days from the date on which you sign it.

Need an accountability partner? If so, complete the *Financial Intimacy 90-Day Letter* online: www.sterlingchoices.net/fi_90dayletter.html. Your letter will be sent back to you ninety days from the date we receive it. Please note: your e-mail address will *never* be shared with a third party and the contents of your letter will be held in the strictest confidence.

Appendix B

Suggested Workbooks, Reading List, and Personal Finance Software

Workbooks

The Motley Fool Personal Finance Workbook: A Foolproof Guide to Organizing Your Cash and Building Wealth by David and Tom Gardner

"Stop Treating Your Money So Poorly Workbook" by Jacquette M. Timmons, a companion to the workshop of the same name

Reading List

The Richest Man in Babylon by George S. Clason

The 7 Habits of Highly Effective People by Stephen R. Covey

Your Money or Your Life: Transforming Your Relationship with Money and Achieving Financial Independence by Joe Dominguez and Vicki Robin

The Secret Code of the Superior Investor: How to Be a Long-Term Winner in a Short-Term World by James Glassman

The Intelligent Investor: The Definitive Book on Value Investing. A Book of Practical Counsel by Benjamin Graham, Jason Zweig, and Warren E. Buffet

Think and Grow Rich by Napoleon Hill

Freakonomics: A Rogue Economist Explores the Hidden Side of Everything by Steven D. Levitt and Stephen J. Dubner

One Up on Wall Street: How to Use What You Already Know to Make Money in the Market by Peter Lynch

Creating Money: Attracting Abundance by Sanaya Roman and Duane Packer

Is the American Dream Killing You?: How "The Market" Rules our Lives by Paul Stiles

Personal Finance Software

Quicken (Quicken Deluxe is my personal favorite)

Mint.com

Appendix C
The Power and Influence of Habits

Habit #1: Track Your Money

Habit #2: Establish and Follow Financial Policies

Habit #3: Save Before You Pay Your Bills

Habit #4: Decide What You Are Going to Save in Advance

Habit #5: Give Your Savings a Purpose

Habit #6: Tie Your Investment Choices to Your Savings Purpose

Habit #7: Track Your Time

Habit #8: Make Stress Your Friend

Habit #9: Follow the Universal Principle of Giving and Receiving

Habit #10: Know Your Credit Score

Habit #11: Delegate, but Don't Abdicate

Habit #12: Don't Count What You Do Not Have

Habit #13: Protect Yourself

Habit #14: Find Your Rhythm, Don't Simply Follow a Routine

Habit #15: Get Some Rest

Habit #16: Schedule Daily Quiet Time

Habit #17: Practice Gratitude

Habit #18: Give Yourself Credit for What You Do Well

Appendix D

The Advisor Questionnaire

$\mathcal{T}$he questions that follow are intended to help you assess the compatibility between you and your potential advisor and to ensure that you have an understanding of the advisor's investment philosophy and approach.

The questions are segmented into two categories: compatibility (fifteen questions) and competency and practice management (ten questions). Though it is not necessary that you ask the potential advisor every question, it is imperative that you lead with the compatibility-oriented questions. There is no point in addressing the mechanics of an advisor's practice if you are not on the same page philosophically! You want to lead with the questions that contribute the most to a successful client/advisor relationship.

Compatibility
1. What does it take to be a great client for you?
2. Who is your ideal client?
3. What's the worst client experience you have had, and what made it so?
4. What's the best client experience you have had, and what made it so?

5. How are we going to measure our progress?
6. What methods of communication do you prefer (phone, e-mail, fax), and how often?
7. How do I fit your client profile?
8. As your business grows and you acquire additional clients, how will you ensure that my account remains your priority?
9. What is the average length of time that you have maintained relationships with your clients?
10. Describe a few of the ways in which you have recently helped a client.
11. When we disagree or you recommend something that I do not want to do, how will you manage that experience?
12. If our relationship does not work to my satisfaction, how do we end it?
13. Beyond the alarm, what makes you get up in the morning?
14. How did you come to the place where you are now in your career?
15. How do you nurture and maintain successful relationships?

Competency and Practice Management

1. How long have you worked in the financial services industry?
2. How long have you been managing money?
3. How will you decide upon the investment strategy you recommend to me?
4. How do you get compensated?
5. Is part of your compensation from any of the managers/mutual funds that you recommend?
6. What's your educational background?
7. Tell me about your support team.
8. Is our investment management relationship discretionary (the advisor can make investment decisions without your involvement or express consent) or nondiscretionary (the advisor needs your express consent before taking any action)?
9. What will you do if an investment does poorly?
10. Will I receive an Investment Policy Statement?

$\mathcal{N}otes$

Introduction

1   http://www.bls.gov/news.release/pdf/nlsoy.pdf

Chapter 1: Other People's Stories

1   Current Population Survey, U.S. Department of Labor, U.S. Bureau of Labor Statistics, 2006. Sixty-three million excludes those who are single due to separation, divorce, or death; if you include people with these statuses, the number increases to 95.7 million.

2   Felicia R. Lee, "Influential Study on Divorce's Impact Is Said to Be Flawed," *New York Times*, May 9, 1996.

3   Joy Bennett Kinnon, "The Shocking State of Black Marriage: Experts Say Many Will Never Get Married," *Ebony*, November 2003.

4   E. J. Graff, "The Opt-Out Myth," *Columbia Journalism Review*, March/April 2007, p. 51.

5   Migrationinformation.org

6   U.S. Census Bureau's Current Population Survey data gathered between 2003 and 2005 show that about 7.5 percent of all marriages are interracial.

7   Milton M. Gordon, 1964. *Assimilation in American Life: The Role of Race, Religion, and National Origins.* New York: Oxford University Press.

8   Bureau of the Public Debt, U.S. Department of the Treasury.

9   The number rose from 3.6 million in 1950 to 5.5 million in 1970. James R. Wetzel, "American Families: 75 Years of Change," *Monthly Labor Review*, March 1990, p. 5.

10   U.S. Department of Health and Human Services, Volume III, Marriage and Divorce, Vital Statistics of the United States, 1969 and 1971.

11   Bureau of Labor Statistics report, "Dual-earner families by number of earners and type of family, 1967–2005."

12   Tamar Lewin, "When Richer Weds Poorer, Money Isn't the Only Difference," *New York Times*, May 19, 2005.

13   David Popenoe and Barbara Dafoe Whitehead, "Should We Live Together?—What Young Adults Need to Know About Cohabitation before Marriage, A Comprehensive Review of Recent Research," Second Edition for the National Marriage Project: Rutgers University.

14   Tamar Lewin, "Boy's Talk of His Gay Mothers Sets Off Furor at His School," *New York Times*, December 3, 2003.

15   Tavia Simmons and Martin O'Connell, U.S. Department of Commerce, U.S. Census Bureau, Married-Couple and Unmarried Partner Households, Census 2000 Special Reports, CEN-SR-5, February 2003, p. 4, tab 2.

16   Gary J. Gates, the Williams Institute, "Same-Sex Couples with the Gay, Lesbian, Bisexual Population: New Estimates from the American Community Survey," p. 11, apx. 1.

17   Adam P. Romero, Amanda K. Baumle, M. V. Lee Badgett, and Gary J. Gates, United States Census Snap shot, the Williams Institute, December 2007.

18   Lynn D. Wardle, Mark Strasser, William C. Duncan, and David Orgon Coolidge, "Marriage and Same-Sex Unions: A Debate," p. 11.

19   Matt Viser, "Gay Marriage Advocates Hope to Repeal Old Law," *Boston Globe*, July 10, 2008.

20   Dr. Gary J. Gates, The Williams Institute, "Same-sex Couples and the Gay, Lesbian, Bisexual Population: New Estimates from the American Community Survey," p. 11, apx. 1, available at http://www.law.ucla.edu/williaminstitute/publications/SameSexCouplesandGLBpopACS.pdf.

21   Marc Gunther, "How Corporate America fell in love with gays and lesbians. It's a movement," *Fortune*, November 30, 2006.

22   Dr. M. V. Lee Badgett. 2001. *Money, Myths, and Change: The Economic Lives of Lesbians and Gay Men*. Chicago: University of Chicago Press.

23   Gayle B. Ronan, "For Love and Money," DanceRetailerNews.com, February 2007, p. 38.

24   Dan Hurley, "Divorce Rate: It's Not as High as You Think," *New York Times*, April 19, 2005.

25   "The Self-Supporting Woman in Oregon: Report on an Inquiry into Her Economic Living Pattern," a study conducted by the State of Oregon Bureau of Labor in the mid-1960s.

26 Libertad Gonzalez (Universitat Pompeu Fabra and IZA Bonn) and Tarja K. Vitanen (University of Sheffield), "The Effect of Divorce Laws on Divorce Rates in Europe," Institute for the Study of Labor, Discussion Paper No. 2023, March 2006, p. 8.

27 New Mexico Commission on the Status of Women, "Women and Divorce, Understanding Your Credit."

28 Libertad Gonzalez (Universitat Pompeu Fabra and IZA Bonn) and Tarja K. Vitanen (University of Sheffield), "The Effect of Divorce Laws on Divorce Rates in Europe," Institute for the Study of Labor, Discussion Paper No. 2023, March 2006, p. 1.

29 Source: U.S. Census Bureau

30 Source: U.S. National Center for Health Statistics Vital Statistics of the United States, annual; and National Vital Statistics Reports (NVSR) (formerly Monthly Vital Statistics Report). The 4.0 figure excludes data for California, Colorado, Indiana, and Louisiana. The latest year which included all states is 1998; at that time the rate was 4.2, not 4.0.

$\mathcal{I}nde x$

Lehman Brothers: bankruptcy of, 173

lending industry: deregulation of, 174

leverage, 177, 179

Lewin, Tamar, 42, 44

liabilities, 123, 130; as "bad" debt, 128; and credit cards, 129; as "good" debt, 128; and personal mortgage, 129

liquidity, 177

Louisiana: divorce rate in, 207n30

love: and money, vii, viii, x, 21, 53–54, 147

Love Jones (film), 78

marriages, 54; changes in, 26; and cross-class, 42–44; and divorce, 76; failure of, reasons for, 73; financial problems, 73; spouse, death of, 87

Massachusetts, 62–63

mates: ATM machines, use of, 153; charities, donations to, 155; and credit score, 155; and death, 90–93; Debt Square, 154; and earning, 158, 160; and expenses, 152; and financial intimacy, 149–51; financial policies, 152; and Financial Wheel, 110, 156, 158–60, 162; investment decisions, 153–54, 157, 159; and money, 166; Pyramid of Wise Money Management, 160–61, 162; qualities in, 4; saving habits of, 153, 156–57; spending habits of, 158–60

merchant banks, 98

Merrill Lynch, 173

"Model of Income in the Near Term (MINT) Project," 8

money, 44; accounting side of, 64; anxiety over, 166; and childhood, xvii; choices, managing of, xv, xviii, xix, 119; and control, 178; and discipline, 102; duality of, 137; earning of, 99, 101–2; emotional impact of, xiii, xv, xviii, 27; and family dynamics, 112–14; financial modes of, 107; and financial policies, 119; financial self-awareness, 118; friction over, 23, 27; giving and receiving of, 137–38; and goals, 130–31; and honesty, 54–55; and identity, xviii; and interdependence, 11; investing of, 99–101, 179–80; and love, vii, viii, x, 21, 53–54, 147; managing of, xviii, 23, 119; mechanics of, as unchanging, 98; nature of, xvii; as personal development tool, 102; power of, 37; as private, x; proactive approach to, 102; psychology side of, 64, 99; purpose of, xviii; reactive approach to, 102; relationship with, 98; and relationships, vii, ix, xvii, 77–78, 165, 167–68; rituals, use of, 168; and savings, 99–100, 102, 119–23, 179; and self-control, 102; as self-revelatory, 86; and social class, 40; spending of, 99, 101; spending of, control over, 180–81; and stress, 80, 133–36; styles of, 78–80; as taboo, 97; time, managing of, 131–33; two sides of, 64

Money, Myths, and Change (Badgett), 68

mortgage debt, 21

multiculturalism, xii

multitasking, 142

mutual funds, xii; and cash allocation, 127; and expense ratio,